URBAN LANGUAGE SERIES

ROGER W. SHUY, GENERAL EDITOR

THE SOCIAL STRATIFICATION OF ENGLISH
IN NEW YORK CITY
WILLIAM LABOV

CONVERSATIONS IN A NEGRO AMERICAN DIALECT
TRANSCRIBED & EDITED BY
BENGT LOMAN

FIELD TECHNIQUES IN AN URBAN LANGUAGE STUDY
ROGER W. SHUY
WALTER A. WOLFRAM
WILLIAM K. RILEY

FIELD TECHNIQUES IN AN

URBAN LANGUAGE STUDY

ROGER W. SHUY

WALTER A. WOLFRAM

WILLIAM K. RILEY

CENTER FOR APPLIED LINGUISTICS : 1968

INTRODUCTION TO THE SERIES

The Urban Language Series is intended to make available the
results of recent sociolinguistic research concerned with the
position and role of language in a large metropolitan area.
The series includes descriptions of certain aspects of urban
language, particularly English, as well as theoretical considerations relevant to such descriptions. The series also includes studies dealing with fieldwork techniques, matters of
pedagogy and relationships of urban language study to other
disciplines. Where appropriate and feasible, accompanying
tape recordings will be made available. Specifically excluded
from consideration are aspects of English as a second language
or second language learning in general.

It is hoped that the Urban Language Series will prove useful to several different kinds of readers. For the linguist,
the series will provide data for the study of language performance and for the development of linguistic theory. Histor-
ically, linguists have formulated theory from individual
rather than group performance. They have had to generalize
about what constitutes "standard" or "non-standard" from intu-
itive judgments or from very limited data. This series is
designed to make available large portions of language data as
well as analyses in order to broaden the knowledge from which
linguistic generalizations may come.

For the sociologist the series will provide access to
the nature of social stratification by means of language. It

is the contention of some scholars that a person's use of language is one of the most important cues to his social status, age, race or sex.

For the educator, the series will offer among other things a description of the very things which are most crucial to the classroom—the linguistic correlates which separate the accepted from the unaccepted.

Although the value of focussed attention on the special problems of urban language has been recognized for some time, relatively few substantial studies have been published. To a certain degree, this series represents a pioneering venture on the part of the Center for Applied Linguistics.

Roger W. Shuy
Director, Sociolinguistics Program
Center for Applied Linguistics

FIELD TECHNIQUES IN AN URBAN LANGUAGE STUDY

PREFACE

THIS VOLUME is essentially a report of the methodology employed in the survey of Detroit speech carried out in 1966-67 by the staff of the Detroit Dialect Study. The research was done through Michigan State University under contract with the Cooperative Research Branch of the U.S. Office of Education. As a methodological study, this work is generally descriptive rather than theoretical in order to provide a practical base for large-scale urban language study. Principles of fieldwork have been accentuated but seemingly trivial details are also included since the authors feel that such details are essential to successful fieldwork.

The following description is not necessarily to be considered as a model for all future fieldwork in urban areas. It is, rather, the embodiment of one approach to the problems posed by large-scale research projects in sociolinguistics. The Detroit study realized at least some of the dimensions of the problems in research of this sort and proposed certain answers to these problems. It is hoped that future research projects will build on this work.

In September 1967, the final report of the Detroit Dialect Study was submitted to the U.S. Office of Education, at which time the data (tape recordings, field transcriptions and demographic materials) were transferred to the Center for Applied Linguistics in Washington, D.C., where they are now housed. Further analyses of these data are currently being carried out by the staff of the Sociolinguistics Program of the Center for Applied Linguistics, and various publications are forthcoming in the Urban Language Series.

The authors are indebted to many people for their assistance during the planning, execution and writing of this study. To our informants, anonymous but greatly appreciated, we owe special thanks. We are also indebted to the field-workers, who contributed particularly during the fieldwork training sessions; Dana Downing, who developed the social status scale; and Edward N. Adams, who was responsible for the computer programming. Invaluable editorial assistance have been generously provided by Frank A. Rice and Allene Guss of the Center for Applied Linguistics.

R.W.S.
Washington, D.C.
July 1968

CONTENTS

Introduction to the Series   v

Preface   ix

1: General Aims   1

2: Sampling Procedures   4

3: Fieldwork Design   20

4: Fieldworker Orientation   29

5: The Questionnaire   39

6: Fieldwork   58

7: Fieldwork Evaluation   115

1: GENERAL AIMS

Sociologists, psychologists, educators, and others have
suggested a number of indices of social stratification,
based on such factors as a person's occupation, education,
attitudes, abilities, and the like. But to the linguist
none of these indices seems as significant as an index
based on a person's use of language, for not only does
language underly the very structure of communication, but
it also frequently lies beneath the surface of consciousness.

In March 1966, the Detroit Dialect Study, under a
contract with the U.S. Office of Education administered
by Michigan State University, embarked upon an investigation
aimed at discovering the linguistic correlates of social
stratification in Detroit speech. The broad objectives of
the Study were:

(1) To describe the specialized linguistic features
of the various English speaking sub-cultures of
Detroit. At the 1964 Conference on Social
Dialects and Language Learning in Bloomington,
Indiana, linguists, sociologists and educators
agreed that a sound procedure for any kind of
English language engineering must begin with the
actual speech of the various classes, age groups,
races, occupation groups and in-migrants. Once
the phonology, grammar, and lexicon have been

adequately described, pedagogical applications can
be made with efficiency and accuracy.

(2) To determine the most efficient methods of language
data gathering in an urban area. It is clear that
each urban area is a complex of various in-migrations
and social layerings. The speech situation in
Detroit, for example, is quite different from that
of other metropolitan areas. This is not to say,
however, that similar techniques of linguistic data
gathering cannot be used in various urban areas. A
second objective in this investigation was to determine which methods of linguistic fieldwork are most
productive with which types of informants, and to
discover what combinations of techniques will be
most useful in the study of a large urban area.

(3) To determine effective methods of language data
storage, retrieval and analysis. The analytical
procedures of a large-scale project of this sort
must necessarily vary from those more commonly
known in linguistic studies. With a large number
of informants who are urged to use different oral
styles, the problems of linguistic bookkeeping
become vast. A significant phase of this research
was devoted to establishing adequate analytical
procedures, both manual and electronic.

(4) To provide accurate and useful language data upon
which educational applications can be based.
Educators are aware of the fact that it is better
to know the systematic structure of the speech of
various sub-cultures than to have only anecdotal
awareness of it. It is better to see the contrastive
patterns of the standard and non-standard speakers
(whether native or in-migrant), and to teach

accordingly, than to engineer individual features
in or out. Furthermore, it is important that educators not waste time teaching against features
which do not actually exist.

To contrast the speech of the so-called disadvantaged
with that of the more socio-economically successful, the
study established a research design which had the following
requirements:

(1) Randomly selecting approximately 700 Detroit resi-
     dents, newcomers and natives, of four major age
     groups from an enumerated population providing as
     few biases as possible.

(2) Interviewing all of these randomly selected people
     with a standard questionnaire which yielded at
     least three styles of speech:

     (a) Conversational (largely narrative and descrip-
          tive) style.

     (b) Single response style. (Short answer responses
          to questions designed to elicit short answers).

     (c) Reading style.

(3) Securing background information about each informant
     (sex, race, age, birthplace, amount of education,
     etc.) which enables the research to correlate speech
     with social stratification.

(4) Analyzing linguistic data and correlating it with
     sociological information.

2: SAMPLING PROCEDURES

Before data gathering for the Detroit Dialect Study could begin, it was necessary to establish a viable research design. Careful attention was paid to matters of sampling, fieldworker orientation, field procedures, and developing a questionnaire.

The Base Sample

The Study took for granted the notion that although the major part of the investigation was linguistic, a part of it was also sociological. One area in which sociological expertise is crucial is sampling: the sample drawn for the Detroit Dialect Study had as one of its objectives to provide a cross section of the people of Detroit. The geographical distribution finally used was chosen on the basis of the assumption that these geographical boundaries represented social boundaries as well. The work of urban sociologists, whose divisions of Detroit related social stratification to geography, was used as a point of departure. The U.S. Census tract figures on income and race seemed to bear out Gerhard Lenski's divisions of Detroit, and the sample was constructed on the basis of his map[1].

Lenski divided Detroit and its suburbs into fourteen areas, nine of which fall within the boundaries of Metropolitan Detroit,

---

[1] Gerhard E. Lenski, The Religious Factor (New York: Doubleday, 1961).

on the basis of ethnicity and religion. He distinguished
four major groups--white Catholics, white Protestants, Negro
Protestants, and Jews--of which one group represented at least
forty and frequently sixty per cent of the population of each
geographical area. For example, the area marked <u>outer city
central</u> was predominantly Jewish; the two inner city areas
were overwhelmingly Negro and Protestant. Taking the nine
areas within the city limits of Detroit--inner city east,
inner city west, middle city east, middle city west, outer
city east, outer city central, outer city west, and the
enclaves Hamtramck and Highland Park--it was found that only
one, Highland Park, straddled Woodward Avenue, which had been
pointed out as an important social boundary in Detroit. Because the investigators were interested in testing the Woodward
Avenue hypothesis from a linguistic point of view, Highland
Park was split into Highland Park East and Highland Park West,
with Woodward Avenue as the dividing line. (As it turned out,
this oversampling of Highland Park was valuable in that it gave
one area of the city in depth, to serve as a check on sampling
procedures in general.) Including both halves of Highland Park
and the other eight areas, there were ten areas of Detroit
from which to draw a geographical stratified sample, or "Base
Sample" (See Map, p. 6).

To select families with children from these ten areas,
a procedure was formulated for drawing at random from the
elementary schools in each area. (A random sample of all
Detroit would have been the prime desideratum, had it been
feasible at the time.) In random sampling, each person in the
total population sampled must have an equal chance of being
selected for the sample. Any deviation from this may affect
the reliability of the research unless it is carefully controlled or accounted for. The procedures of the Study were
designed to minimize the effect of such biases.

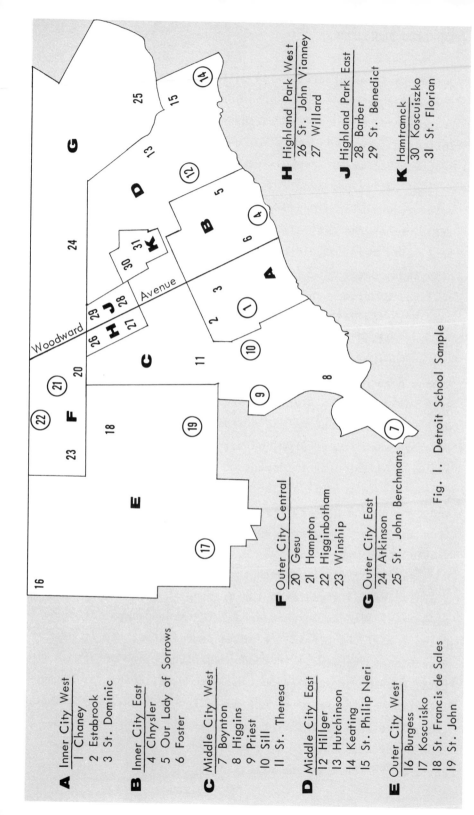

A Inner City West
  1 Chaney
  2 Estabrook
  3 St. Dominic

B Inner City East
  4 Chrysler
  5 Our Lady of Sorrows
  6 Foster

C Middle City West
  7 Boynton
  8 Higgins
  9 Priest
  10 Sill
  11 St. Theresa

D Middle City East
  12 Hillger
  13 Hutchinson
  14 Keating
  15 St. Philip Neri

E Outer City West
  16 Burgess
  17 Koscuisko
  18 St. Francis de Sales
  19 St. John

F Outer City Central
  20 Gesu
  21 Hampton
  22 Higginbotham
  23 Winship

G Outer City East
  24 Atkinson
  25 St. John Berchmans

H Highland Park West
  26 St. John Vianney
  27 Willard

J Highland Park East
  28 Barber
  29 St. Benedict

K Hamtramck
  30 Koscuiszko
  31 St. Florian

Fig. 1. Detroit School Sample

At the suggestion of consultants for sampling procedure, the investigators decided to work through the elementary schools, though with the realization that this decision automatically biased the sample against childless people and people whose children were either too young or too old for elementary school. First, all the public and parochial schools in each of Lenski's areas were listed separately, and then one public and one parochial school were drawn at random in each area. (See Fig. 1, Detroit School Sample, p. 6.)

Drawing the Samples

From each Base Sample school, 30 names were selected at random. This was done by obtaining for each school the total of all children in the fourth, fifth, and sixth grades, and dividing that total by 30. This gave the ratio number for selection per grade. For example, if in a particular school there were 100 children in fourth, 100 in fifth, and 100 in sixth grade, every tenth name per grade was picked. If there were 200 in fourth, 50 in fifth, and 50 in sixth, then every twentieth name in fourth, every fifth name in fifth, and every fifth name in sixth were chosen from the alphabetized class lists. From the resulting list of 30 names, 10 were chosen for the sample.

For each Ethnic Sample school, (see pg. 9) the same procedure was followed, but the total was divided by 15, and from the resulting list, 5 were chosen.

Just over one-half of the schools selected for the Base and Ethnic Samples combined were Detroit public schools. Because of a school regulation, addresses could not be obtained from the school files; instead, letters had to be sent home to parents with return envelopes containing their addresses. This requirement caused a slightly different procedure to be used for these schools than for the other schools in the sample. The other schools--the private schools of Detroit, and the public schools of Hamtramck and Highland Park--were amenable to a simpler procedure. The two procedures can be outlined as follows:

Procedure followed in private schools and Hamtramck and Highland Park Public Schools: From the thirty (or fifteen) names obtained, every third name was selected, beginning with fourth grade and ending with sixth. The administrative assistant of the Study went to these homes and made an appointment for an interview. If the people chosen in this way were not available (gone for the summer, moved away, seriously ill, or unwilling), the administrative assistant went to the top of the list, choosing the top fourth grader first, the top fifth grader second, the top sixth grader third, the second fourth grader fourth, and so on. This was done except in a very few cases in which the names were taken out of order for some reason.

Procedure followed in Detroit Public Schools: In most cases, at least ten of the thirty (or five of the fifteen) parents of Detroit public school children returned cards with addresses. In each case, interviews were obtained from this list, in an attempt to comply with the requirements of the system. Some schools had more cards returned than others. If twenty cards were retrieved in a school requiring ten names, every other card, in alphabetical order, was chosen. If one of the ten selected in this way were unavailable or unwilling, the administrative assistant went to the top of the stack of remaining names, working from top to bottom.

The Ethnic Sample

At this point it became clear that certain areas of possible linguistic interest which had been brought to the attention of the investigators were not covered by the Base Sample: the west Detroit Polish section, the areas inhabited by recent white in-migrants from the South, some middle class Negro neighborhoods, and such anomalies as schools which were attended by poor Negro and well-to-do white children. To supplement the stratified sample, the investigators decided to draw a judgment sample based on information about sociologically interesting areas of Detroit that were not included in the Base Sample. The schools chosen were located at the center of eleven such areas, and the same procedure used for the Base Sample; however, fewer informants were drawn from each school. The sample thus drawn was called the Ethnic Sample (See Map, p. 6).

In cases where fewer cards were returned than interviews required, all of the returned cards were used; for example, where only eight were returned, those eight were selected and the remaining 22 names were divided by the number needed (2). Thus, every eleventh card was selected.

In one school, only one card was returned. In this school, the private school procedure was followed.

In every family selected, the Study interviewed at least two people: the child whose name had been drawn at the elementary school, and one of his parents or acting parents. This gave a basic two-generational depth useful for studies of language acquisition. In addition, a third generation and on rare occasions a fourth were added when interviews could be scheduled with grandparents and great-grandparents in the Detroit area. Moreover, wherever possible, a teen-age sibling of the elementary school child was interviewed to see if there

were any significant changes in adolescent speech. Finally,
in the three instances where the family selected contained a
set of twins, both were interviewed.

Several biases were recognized from the outset and can
be regarded as controlled as long as they are taken into consideration in the analysis. They include the following:

(1) Parochial heaviness. According to 1965 statistics,
     approximately one elementary school child in four
     was enrolled in Detroit parochial schools. The Base
     Sample allows for 50% parochial representation.

(2) Willingness of participants. Of the 30 (or 15)
     names randomly selected in each public school, in-
     formants were drawn only from the list of those who
     willingly returned address cards.

(3) Parental Imbalance. Various considerations caused
     the sample to include mothers far more frequently
     than fathers. Availability and willingness were
     strong factors here, but it must be recalled also
     that the matrifocal family is common in the inner
     city.

(4) Localness. In other kinds of random sampling from
     the same areas it would be unlikely that 50 to 70
     informants would be chosen from the same two school
     districts. Although all elementary school children
     initially stood the same chance of being selected,
     only a limited number were still eligible once the
     schools were selected.

(5) Homogeneity. Only those families with children in
     the upper elementary grades were included in the
     sample. Childless adults and parents of children
     in other age groups were not eligible.

When completed, the sample contained 702 interviews in
31 school districts and over 250 families. (In only seven

instances did the randomly selected informants decline to be
interviewed.) Almost all the biases in the sampling were
directly due to the differences between the type of information
the sociologist requires and the kind of data that interest the
linguist. For example, only infrequently would a sociologist
want a sample to include three people from each family; he
would probably be satisfied with one. But the linguist's interest in the influences of parental and peer-group speech on
the child make both this bias and the bias of localness useful,
not detrimental to the study.

Social Stratification of Sample

The correlation of social status and linguistic performance first requires a careful delineation of each. That is,
before it is possible to make any statements about "working
class" or "professional" speech, it is necessary to rank all
informants on objective, non-linguistic criteria.

The following section contains the procedures used by
the Study for the social classification of informants. There
are several available models for deriving some sort of quanti-
fiable indication of social status. After consultation with
sociologists, the model chosen for this research was an adaptation of the procedure outlined in Appendix II of August
Hollingshead's Social Class and Mental Illness (1958)[2]. Three
factors are used to evaluate social status: residence, education, and occupation. In order to rank an individual, one
needs to know his job, how many years of school he has had,
and what kind of neighborhood he lives in. Hollingshead used
a pre-existing survey of housing in his study of New Haven;
the Detroit Dialect Study had only the U.S. Census data from

---

[2]The authors are indebted to Dana Downing for much of this
adaptation and analysis.

which to derive a ranking system. With this exception,
Hollingshead's procedure was followed exactly.

The educational scale is as follows:

Class	Level of Education
1	Any graduate degree (professional)
2	College graduation (four-year)
3	One year or more of college
4	High school graduation
5	Some high school (tenth grade up)
6	Junior high school (seventh through ninth
7	Less than seven years of school

(Attendance at business college or some sort of training
institute was not taken as equivalent to attendance at a college or junior college.)

The occupational scale requires the use of Alba Edwards'
Alphabetical Index of Occupations and Industries (1940), with
certain updating from consulting sociologists. The breakdown
is as follows:

Class	Occupation
1	Major professionals Executives of large concerns
2	Lesser professionals Executives of medium-sized concerns
3	Semi-professionals Administrators of small businesses
4	Technicians Owners of petty businesses
5	Skilled workmen
6	Semi-skilled workmen
7	Unskilled workers

There were a few difficulties in applying Edwards' Index,
as Hollingshead was not explicit as to what constituted a
"lesser professional," or on where the protective service
workers were to be classed in this system. Protective workers
and service workers were treated as semi-skilled, unless they
had extra responsibilities (a detective sergeant was grouped
with the foremen and skilled workmen, for instance). But the
system was generally unambiguous and easy to manipulate.

Finally, there was the difficulty of ranking residence
by the Census data. In order to use as much of the Census
data as possible, a fairly complex procedure was worked out.
First, each informant was placed on the 1960 block census,
i.e., by means of the City Directory and the street address,
it was determined on which block he lived, and he was assigned
a block and tract number. Then, for each of the tracts in which
the informants lived, a rating was determined. From the Housing
Census, it was discovered how many of the houses in the tract
were sound and had all plumbing facilities. The tracts were
then grouped on the basis of this percentage. Group A included
those tracts in which at least 98% of the houses were sound
with all plumbing; Group B, 87.5%; Group C, 66.6%; Group D,
50%; and Group E, under 50%. Each group was then further sub-
divided by the number of rooms per house in the tract. Subgroup
1 included the tracts where the average number of rooms was
at least 10.5; Subgroup 2, 7.5-10.4; Subgroup 3, 5.5-7.4;
Subgroup 4, 4.5-5.4; and Subgroup 5, 4.4 or under. Then the
subclasses were regrouped into six categories to follow
Hollingshead's breakdown into six residency types. Table 1
shows the classification matrix.

The median family income figure for each tract was taken
from the population census, and a median of these medians was
found for Classes I through VI. The medians correlated with
position on the scale, with a top of $14,220 for Class I and

Table 1

Classification Matrix

Percentage of Houses With Sound Plumbing
In Census Block

No. Rooms Per Occupied Unit		98% - 97.9% A	87.5% - 87.4% B	66.6% - 66.5% C	50% - D	under 50% E
10.5 -	1	I	I	II	III	IV
7.5-10.4	2	I	II	III	IV	V
5.5-7.4	3	II	III	IV	V	VI
4.5-5.4	4	III	IV	V	VI	VI
4.4 & under	5	IV	V	VI	VI	VI

a low of $3,582 for Class VI. The average value of houses
also showed a close correlation.

Next, the same classification was done for the individual
blocks in which the informants lived. One modification was
made: Group A included only those blocks in which 100% of the
houses were sound and had all plumbing facilities. The classification proceeded as above, into Classes I-VI. Then the
median family income for the tract in which the block was located was compared with the median of median family incomes
for the classification by tracts into Classes I-VI. If it

exceeded the median by $2,000 or more, the block moved up
into the next class (IV to III, for instance); and if it was
$2,000 or more below the median, the block was moved down one
class. Classes I through VI were then used as an equivalent
of Hollingshead's six-point scale for residence. The Brewster
Projects, low cost, government subsidized housing areas,
received an automatic VI classification.

At this point, each informant had three rating numbers:
(a) a rating from one to seven on education; (b) a rating from
one to seven on occupation; and (c) a rating from one to six
on residence. These numbers were then multiplied by factors
of 5, 9, and 6, respectively, the sum of these numbers being
the informant's position on the scale. For instance, a law-
yer who lived in a Class I neighborhood would receive a 1
for education, a 1 for occupation, and a 1 for residence.
Multiplied by 5, 9, and 6 respectively, these give a combined
score of 20. For a person rated 7 on both education and occupation (a laborer with a third grade education, for example),
with a house in a Class VI neighborhood, the score is 134.
Obviously, the lower the number the higher the prestige, and
vice versa. (Displays of general social information on families in each school area were prepared. One such display
appears on page 19.)

The above procedure was not used for the Hamtramck
district, since the 1960 block census of housing did not cover
it. Therefore, only the median family income figures were
available. In this case, the medians for the classification
by tracts into Classes I-VI were used. Class I, with a
median of $14,220, had a range of $10,000 to $18,440; all
tracts with a median family income of $10,000 or more were
rated as Class I, for the purpose of rating tracts in
Hamtramck. The complete listing is as follows:

Class	Median	Range: Median Family Income		Hamtramck
I	$14,220	$10,000 to	$18,440	$10,000 and up
II	9,213	9,026 to	12,926	8,000 - 9,999
III	6,362	5,111 to	8,809	6,350 - 7,999
IV	6,327	4,254 to	7,648	5,500 - 6,349
V	4,713	4,085 to	6,008	4,300 - 5,499
VI	3,582	1,879 to	4,440	4,299 and under

Once all the families were ranked by this system, conclusions about the relationship of language and social class could be drawn.

In order to show the range of socio-economic levels which were obtained in the sample, four different types of graphs showing the distribution of informants by social status were prepared (See Figs. 2-5).

Charting the distribution of informants in terms of their relative status has a twofold purpose. It serves, first, to indicate whether the study adequately represents the spectrum of socio-economic differences, from the lowest to highest social status levels. The distribution of the White Base population indicates a fairly representative distribution, except for the lower social status scores, where the representation is somewhat sparse. The combination of the Base and Ethnic sample for the white population does not really change the distribution in any significant way. The distribution of the Negro Base population, as might be expected, shows a completely different distribution. The Base sample shows the concentration of informants at the lower end (i.e., with higher numerical scores) of the social status scale, so that the middle class

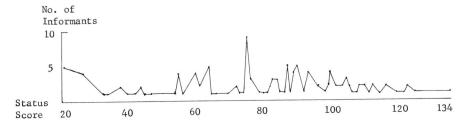

Fig. 2: Social Distribution of White Base Sample

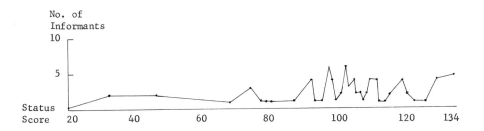

Fig. 3. Social Distribution of Negro Base Sample

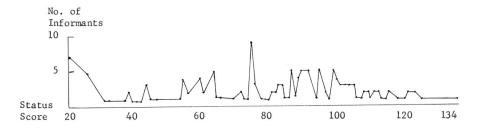

Fig. 4. Social Distribution of White Base and Ethnic Sample

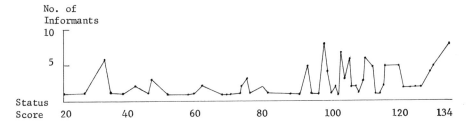

Fig. 5. Social Distribution of Negro Base and Ethnic Sample

Negro population is not represented in sufficient quantities for analysis. This apparent deficiency is compensated for when the Base and Ethnic sample are combined, so that the full continuum of social status differences among the Negro population is adequately represented.

The second purpose of the charting is to gain some impressionistic insight as to where "natural" breaks between scores might occur, thus justifying some breakdown of the social status continuum into discrete "classes." The white population does not show clear-cut divisions in the middle range (78-110), but a clustering of informants at the uppermost end of the continuum and one somewhat lower (55-65) is observed. The Negro Base sample indicates a clustering of informants at the lower end of the social status scale. When the Base and Ethnic samples are combined for the Negro population, a group with relatively high social status (30-40) and one in the middle (60-77) seem to divide themselves from the scores at the lower end of the continuum.

Base Sample Population --- Highland Park East

General Social Information of Families in the Barber School Area

Field-worker	Family & Tape No.	Sex, Age, Race	Highest Educational Level	Occupation	Spouse's Occupation	Social Status
REC	A-0167	F 42 W	C,4	volunteer worker	minister	26
RKS	A-0171	F 10 W	4			
JWN	A-0148*	F 15 W	11			
JL	B-0667	F 38 W	12+		engineer	72
RKS	B-0512	M 9 W	4			
JWN	C-0178	M 42 W	M.A.	teacher	teacher	44
CWJ	C-0179	F 9 W	4			
VHL	C-0192*	F 13 W	8			
REC	D-0225	M 37 N	11+USAF	factory worker		104
WAW	D-0239	M 12 N	6			
CMW	D-0261*	F 14 N	7			
EAA	E-0353	F 32 W	12		bar/restaurant owner	74
VHL	E-0283	F 11 W	5			
REC	F-0222	M 43 W	C,2	restaurant/ hotel owner		54
WKR	F-0295	F 12 W	6			
RKS	F-0344gm	F 64 W	12			
CWJ	G-0577	F 34 W	10	school lunch monitor	janitor	86
JL	G-0548	F 11 W	5			
DD	G-0574	M 11 W	5			
CMW	H-0138	F 42 N	8	house cleaner	pullman porter	105
JL	H-0156	F 10 N	5			
DD	H-0135gm	F 54 N	11			
JL	J-0320	F 49 W	10		mechanic & garage owner	74
WKR	J-0297	M 10 W	6			
JWN	K-0249	F 30 W	C,2½		minister	43
CWJ	K-0310	M 10 W	4			

Code: 0000   Parent   * Older sibling   gm   Grandmother

3: FIELDWORK DESIGN

The Detroit Dialect Study relied heavily on an administrative assistant to secure all interviews. It was assumed that once the informants in the sample were drawn, one person should contact all families, secure permission for the following interview, answer preliminary questions, generally assure the people of their role, and set up a definite appointment for the interview itself.

Selection of the administrative assistant was a crucial matter. A major criterion was adaptability. The position required a person who would be able to convince the prospective informants to permit an interview. Specific knowledge of linguistics was not really as important as congeniality. A beginning assumption was, in fact, that a linguist per se would not be as good for this position as one with personnel experience. Consequently, a person with experience in administrative responsibilities who had done some personnel work was hired. The administrative assistant's background included close dealings with people of all social levels and all ages.

The administrative assistant went to the area of the homes of each of the randomly selected informants and set up interview appointments in person. Gauging the reception or attitude of the informant, she tried to determine what approach to use. One type of statement of how the goals might be presented to the informant would be: "We are interested in how different people talk in this area." Securing an interview took anywhere

from five minutes to an hour, depending on the person's
availability, willingness and attitude toward the project.
In some homes it was necessary to listen to family history,
examine bruises and cuts of the children and exchange recipes.
Occasionally the contact was made away from the home at a
place of business or some other designated area at the request
of the prospective informant. In some cases the administrative
assistant had to return to the home more than once in order
to secure the appointment.

The administrative assistant's reception in the homes
varied. Although all homes were sent a letter preceding her
arrival, not all expected her. Some knew vaguely about the
project but were slightly surprised. Others responded with
little or no awareness of the project.

The administrative assistant's appointment book for time
and work schedule contained information about:

      (a)   The number of workers available that day;

      (b)   Special information about the area (e.g.,
            whether or not evening interviews might
            prove dangerous);

      (c)   Accessibility of the area to the operations
            base.

Depending on the informants' work and living patterns as well
as his availability for interviewing, the administrative
assistant suggested an interview time varying from one day
to six weeks in advance. (On two or three occasions, the
interviews were set up immediately after the contact.) If
the suggested time was acceptable to the informant, the
appointment was confirmed and an appointment card was left
in the home. This card served as a reminder of the appointment and also to give authority to the project and credentials
to the administrative assistant. The sample appointment card
is as follows:

```
┌─────────────────────────────────────────────────────────────┐
│                                                             │
│   Roger W. Shuy, Director                                   │
│   Summer Headquarters                                       │
│   Stouffer's Northland Inn          DETROIT DIALECT STUDY   │
│   357-4700 Room 539                                         │
│      or 357-4108                                           │
│                                                             │
│   in cooperation with the United States Office of          │
│   Education and Michigan State University                  │
│                                                             │
│   School Area_____K eating_____               │
│                                                             │
│   Appointments_Mrs. H—_ Time__July 19___                   │
│         _Quinton_____    __Tues.____                     │
│         _Jeffrey_____   __1:00_____                     │
│                                                             │
│         _____       _____                     │
│                                                             │
└─────────────────────────────────────────────────────────────┘
```

Fig. 6. Sample Appointment Card

Other credentials used by the administrative assistant
to establish rapport included:

(a)   information from the Archdiocese of Detroit (in
      the case of families from Catholic schools);

(b)   information from various school principals (in the
      case of families from public schools);

(c)   Michigan State University credentials: letter from
      Dr. Shuy, Director.

Only infrequently was it necessary to provide the informant
with these special credentials.

Depending on the area, the individual, and whether or
not the person requested a reminder, a follow-up was initiated.
This was either in the form of a telephone call, a visit, or
a postcard. The administrative assistant scheduled an average
of sixteen interviews daily throughout the fieldwork period.
The number varied from day to day, depending on how the informants chose to be scheduled. She also handled cancellations

time changes, rescheduling, and other problems dealing with
the interview.

It was immediately clear that any large scale interview
procedure such as this would need a common operations base.
The director and the administrative assistant investigated
several possibilities and deciced upon a strategically located
hotel as the best choice for a base. The major criteria for
such a selection were:

> (a) Availability throughout the summer on a five
>   day per week basis;
>
> (b) Relatively soundproof rooms for fieldworkers
>   to listen to the tapes and do their phonetic
>   transcriptions;
>
> (c) Accessibility to major Detroit arteries as
>   well as to the Michigan State University
>   home base in East Lansing.

The hotel selected for the operations base, though located
on the northern limits of the city, met these criteria very
well. It was on the major north-south expressway (which
links to the major east-west expressway), it had ample and
relatively quiet accommodations for phonetic analysis, and
the management was agreeable to a five day a week rental
schedule.

The necessity of the single operations base may be clearly
seen in relationship to the following advantages:

> (a) Formal and informal staff meetings were easily
>   arranged, usually in the evenings;
>
> (b) Car pool arrangements were easily made, since
>   all fieldworkers were in the same building;
>
> (c) Accessibility of the director, the tape
>   recording specialist-technician, and the
>   administrative assistant for advice on matters
>   pertaining to them;

(d) Accessibility of other fieldworkers for con-
     sultation concerning special elicitation
     techniques, help on difficult phonetics matters,
     etc.;

(e) The indefinable unity or _esprit de corps_ which
     can develop in group projects of this sort.

The director's room served as the central message deposi-
tory, switchboard and supply room during the fieldwork period.
Completed tapes, phonetic transcriptions, and interview completion cards were turned in to his office daily.

An urban area is always in a state of flux and the longer
the fieldwork is drawn out the more fluctuation will be
included. To get a somewhat accurate picture of Detroit speech
at a given point in time it was decided to complete all fieldwork within approximately ten weeks. In order to finish this
task within such a short period of time, it was necessary to
engage a relatively large team of fieldworkers. Eleven
linguists with rather widely differing professional backgrounds
were chosen for this project. It was also felt that by having
a team of linguists interview and transcribe phonetically,
individual biases in technique and hearing might be minimized.

Since between two and four interviews were done in any
given home, all interviews were scheduled at the same time
and two to four linguists were sent in one car. There were
several distinct advantages to this procedure. First, travel
costs and time were obviously minimized. Secondly, the problem of parents observing (or interfering with) the interview
of their children was avoided. The fieldworkers would go to
different parts of the home for relative separation from other
simultaneous interviews. A typical situation might find the
child being interviewed in the kitchen, a parent in the living
room, and an older sibling in the backyard.

The administrative assistant and the director took
particular care to assign interview teams which had complemen-
tary strengths. Certain fieldworkers, for example, established
themselves as particularly effective at convincing informants
to let the linguists interview them. Occasionally, even after
agreeing to the interview and setting up an appointment, an
informant might become uneasy. If the administrative assistant suspected this characteristic, she would try to assign
the best "interview salvager" to that home. Other fieldworkers
showed special abilities for interviewing older people, children, teenagers, or certain ethnic groups. When possible,
these linguists were assigned to their special strengths
although all fieldworkers had considerable experience with
all types.

The interviews were done in the home or home areas of
the informants. It was felt that the school environment
might unduly slant the informants' speech to a more formal
or "school-type" variety. Home interviews are a bit more
casual and the informant has the distinct advantage of
familiar surroundings. Occasionally, if the informant desired,
or if the home was too noisy, the interview was conducted in
a nearby area.

The evening before a given day's work the administrative
assistant and the director devised fieldwork teams for the
ensuing day based on routing possibilities, fieldworker
specialities, and available drivers. A separate work assignment card for each interview was distributed to the room
of each fieldworker sometime during the evening. Note that
the appointment card and the assignment card were used inter-
changeably but that the assignment card contained special
directions relevant to the fieldworker, including the following information:

THE DETROIT DIALECT STUDY   *REC*

in cooperation with the United States Office of
Education and Michigan State University

School Area _____ *St. John Vianney* _____

Appointments _____ *Mrs. F—* _____

REC _____ *Debbie* _____

WKR _____ *Betsy* _____

RKS _____ *Wed. June 22 — 10:00 a.m.*

Dr. Roger W. Shuy, Director   Summer Headquarters
Phone 517-355-7575   Stouffer's Northland Inn
Michigan State University   Southfield, Michigan
East Lansing, Michigan   357-4700

Fig. 7.   Sample Assignment Card

The initials at the upper right indicated that this card was
for fieldworker REC who would understand from it that he was
to drive (initials underlined on left) and that his passengers
were WKR and RKS. On the back of this card were directions
on how to get to this address and a note that it was a Polish-
Italian family.

At the time indicated on the card, the fieldwork team
assembled in the hotel lobby and left for the interview.
Exact assignments for the members of each family were seldom
made by the director or administrative assistant but after a
few days of interviewing, one could generally guess which
linguist would interview which member of the family.

Each interview was tape recorded using a Uher 4000 L
battery powered portable tape recorder and Scotch Brand mylar
No. 150 tape (900 feet). The portable tape recorder was thought
necessary because many interviews were done on porches,

playgrounds, and backyards; and though all the homes of the
informants had electricity, the number and quality of outlets
was questionable. In simultaneous fieldwork of this sort
maneuverability is of the utmost importance.

Each fieldworker was assigned a tape recorder during
fieldworker training week. It was his responsibility to see
to it that his machine was properly charged, in good mechani-
cal condition and ready for each interview. He was also
responsible for his battery charger, lavaliere microphone,
carrying case and tapes. A twelfth tape recorder was used
by the director to listen to the work of the fieldworkers
and to serve as a substitute when necessary.

The fieldworkers were also responsible for attaching the
leaders to all the tapes and numbering them in advance. On
three occasions during the fieldwork period, the fieldworkers
assembled for a "leadering and numbering" session under the
direction of the fieldworker who doubled as technical assistant.
After each interview the fieldworkers were also responsible
for labeling the tape box, the leader tape and the tape reel.

The entire interview was tape recorded using an Electro-
voice (Model 647A Dynamic, low impedance) lavaliere microphone.
It was hoped that the lavaliere microphone would be less
conspicuous than a table model and therefore would allow for
more casual responses. In general this expectation seemed
to be fulfilled. The lavaliere microphone was also valuable
in that, being close to the informant's mouth, it yielded
rather high quality recordings. On the other hand, the
microphone cord had two disadvantages. First, excessive
handling of the cord produced static. Secondly, the length
of the cord made it an effective antenna for short wave
broadcasts. The microphone clip minimized both problems.

The staff of the Detroit Dialect Study was unanimous in
rejecting the idea of tape recording speech when the informants

were unaware that they were being recorded. Before appointments were made, the administrative assistant explained to
the prospective informants that the interview would be tape
recorded. The linguists made no effort to disguise the tape
recording, usually talking about it before each interview.
No tricks were played on the subjects and no pretense was made
of the fieldworkers being anything but linguists. There were
no hidden microphones or bugged rooms. It was the feeling
of the investigators that the recorded speech was not quite
casual but also not formal. It was a good sample of the
speech used by children to adults (perhaps similar to classroom language) and by adults to respected strangers. It
could seldom be considered in-group speech, particularly for
teenagers or adults. It is, nevertheless, one of the most
important styles of speech used by Americans, for it is
this style in which they make their moves up (or down) the
social scale.

Fieldworkers were advised not to try to do phonetic
transcription during the interview. It was felt that the
interviewer would do well to devote his attention to the
problems of speech elicitation and rapport. Upon completion
of the interview, the fieldworker returned to his hotel room
and transcribed phonetically Section V (the short response
section) of the questionnaire. Then he turned in his tape,
assignment card (initialed next to person interviewed and
noted with tape number) and transcription to the director.

4: FIELDWORKER ORIENTATION

Orientation Schedule

In a project attempting to complete several hundred
interviews within a period of a few weeks, the task of
orienting fieldworkers to the methods and goals of the
research is one of the most essential aspects of the research
design. On the one hand, there is limited time which can be
alloted for such orientation. On the other hand, however, it
is imperative that fieldworkers gain a clear conception of
the goals of the research and the means by which these are
to be realized. Failure in this regard can have major con-
sequences with potential effects on much of the sample. Only
the initial week was set aside for fieldworker orientation
for the Detroit Dialect Study, although several special semi-
nars were held during the course of the fieldwork to discuss
topics omitted or merely touched upon in the initial orientation week. The orientation schedule is shown in Table 2.

Aims of Orientation

The first aim of orientation was to acquaint the fieldworker with the goals of the project and the research design.
The goals of the Study were presented and discussed, comparing
it with the "traditional" dialect geography study and the
more recent urban linguistic studies. Main areas covered
under the presentation and discussion of research were:
(a) the sample; (b) the questionnaire; and (c) the interview.

Table 2. Orientation Schedule

	Monday	Tuesday	Wednesday	Thursday	Friday
8-9	goals of DDS and research design	phonetic drill	phonetic drill	phonetic drill	phonetic drill
9-10		instructions in operation of tape recorder	discussion and modification of phonetic notation system	interview evaluation	accommodation schedule
10-11	hiring procedure	practice interview	discussion of questionnaire		interview evaluation
11-12					
12-1	lunch	lunch	lunch	lunch	lunch
1-2	presentation and discussion of question- naire and interview	presentation and discussion of sample design	practice interview	practice interview	practice interview
2-3		research design and analytical procedure			
3-4	presentation of phonetic notation system		interview evaluation	interview evaluation	interview evaluation
4-5	phonetic drill	phonetic drill	phonetic drill	phonetic drill	phonetic drill

The presentation and discussion of the research design were
considered essential as a basis for understanding the dynamics
of the fieldwork. For example, an understanding of the
selection of the sample stressed the importance of completing
each randomly selected interview in order to minimize selection bias.

The second aim was to familiarize the fieldworkers with
the questionnaire and the style of the interview. This was
done in two ways. First, each question to be asked in the
Discussion section of the questionnaire, and each item to
be elicited in the Short Response section were independently
discussed. In the Discussion section the type of narration
or description which emerge from each question and the adaptation of the questionnaire to elicit the desired narrative
or description was treated; in the Short Response section
the various lexical alternants and the possible definitions
to aid the elicitation of items were treated. Second,
practice interviews were conducted using residents of the
Lansing area as informants. (The orientation program took
place at Michigan State University in East Lansing.) This
provided experience for the fieldworkers in utilizing the
questionnaire in the interview situation; it also aided
in coordinating the various sections of the questionnaire
and the manipulation of the tape recorder in an actual interview situation. In conducting the practice interviews,
each fieldworker was responsible for obtaining his own
informants, and was asked to include representatives of
both sexes, different age levels, and different races in
his samples. The specification of sex, age, and race variables was intended to introduce the fieldworkers to the
different types of problems which might be expected on the
basis of these variables, and to practice adapting the
questionnaire to the different types of informants. The

group listened to and evaluated a portion of each fieldworker's
tape-recorded interview, noting the apparent strengths and
weaknesses of the interview technique. Specific suggestions
on the adaptation of the questionnaire to sex, age, and ethnic
differences emerged from the practice interviews. These interviews also served as a final check on the validity of the
questionnaire and the potential "productivity" or "non-pro-
ductivity" of specific questions and items.

A third aim of the orientation week was the practice
of phonetic transcription, and the adoption of a phonetic
notation system for the transcription. The notational
system adopted is shown in Figs. 8 and 9.

Each day two hours were allotted to phonetic drills,
arranged to sharpen the auditory perception of the fieldworkers prior to the actual fieldwork. (One fieldworker
was assigned as the leader of the phonetics drill although
other fieldworkers assisted in the exercises.) Several
types of exercises were employed to emphasize the types of
phonological differences which might be important in the
research. The first type of exercise consisted of articulatory production, particularly emphasizing vowel production.
It was felt that if a fieldworker had an adequate articulatory
control of the vowel differences which might be anticipated
in Detroit speech, he would be more consistent in his auditory
perception. Each fieldworker's phonetic realization of the
English phonemes was also noted in order to have some idea
of the type of interference one might expect from a fieldworker's dialect.

The second type of exercise consisted of phonetic
transcription, both from dictation by various fieldworkers
and from the tape-recorded sample interviews. Specific
phonetic differences essential to the anticipated analysis
were emphasized in the transcription exercises. For example,

| | Front | | Central | Back | |
	unrounded	rounded	unrounded	unrounded	rounded
High	i	i̭		ṷ	u
Lower-high	ɪ		ɨ		U
Mid	e	ḙ	ə	o̭	o
Lower-mid	ɛ				
Low	æ	æ̭			ɔ
Lower-low	a		ɑ	ɒ	

Modifications:

off-glide	V^i, V^ə, V^u, etc.
on-glide	wV, yV (strong); ^uV, ^iV (weak)
fronted	V<
backed	V>
raised	V^
lowered	Vᵛ
nasalized	Ṽ (strong), V̜
devoiced	V̥
rounded - unrounded	V̭ (extreme); V̲ (slight)
(e.g.: o̭ = o; e̲ = rounded e)	
length	V· (long); V: (extra long)
diphthongs	Vɪ (one peak); Vᶦ (two peaks)
laryngealized	ʔa, ʔi, ʔo, etc.
pharyngealized	a̰, ḭ, o̰, etc.
breathy	a̟, i̟, o̟, etc.
retroflexed	ạ, ị, ọ, etc.

Fig. 8. Vowel Chart

Stops:	p t k ʔ b d g
Affricates:	č ǰ
Fricatives:	f θ s š x v ð z ž
Nasals:	m m› (labio-dental) n ŋ
Laterals:	1^ (high tongue) 1ᵛ (low tongue) ł (velarized)
Flaps:	ť ď
Trills:	Ṛ̃ (voiceless) ṛ̃ (voiced)
Other	w y r

Modifications:

unreleased	C⌐
fronted	C‹
backed	C›
devoiced	C̥
voiceless → voicing	C̰
voiced → devoicing	C̱
aspirated	Cʰ
fricativized	₵
retroflexed	C̣
syllabic consonant	C̦
impediment	C V C̍↓ V (notably present)
	C V C̩↑ V (notably absent)
hesitation	◇

Fig. 9. Consonant Chart

consider the following transcription exercise:

1. a: 'kʰẽⁱ: dɪᵘ ɪt   'I can't do it'
2. weⁱ yɪᵘ 'gõᵘ: 'Where are you going?'
3. arčɪ'fɪšəl   'artificial'
4. ǰanz 'goᵘɪn 'hoᵘm   'John's going home'
5. aⁱgaᵉ: goᵘ 'skuᵘ: 'I gotta go to school'

In the above exercise it should be noted that such phonological features as the loss of r and l, the substitution of a
nasalized vowel for a nasal consonant, and specific vowel and
consonant variants were included to point out essential
differences which the fieldworkers would be expected to per-
ceive and transcribe consistently. At the conclusion of the
week, preliminary impressions of each fieldworker's transcription "accuracy" (i.e., based on the leader's norm) were
noted. (At the conclusion of the fieldwork, a transcription
exercise was again given to compare the transcription of
each fieldworker at the beginning and end of the fieldwork.)

The fourth aim of the orientation was to learn or review
the basic skills of operating the tape recorder during the
interview. Standard procedures for satisfactory and consistent operation of the tape recorders were outlined, and the
information to be included with the submission of each tape
was designated. For example, the information written on the
leader of each tape was to include: (1) the date of the interview; (2) the name of the fieldworker; (3) the number of the
tape recorder used; (4) the informant's name; and (5) tape
number. Details such as the procedures for operating the
tape recorder and the information to be included on each
submitted tape, although seemingly trivial, were essential
to the organizational success of the fieldwork.

The fifth aim of orientation week was simply the estab-
lishment of a working relationship between the fieldworkers.
Preliminary impressions of the various abilities of the
fieldworkers suggested the ways in which the interview teams

were to be sent out, and living accommodations were to be
arranged for the fieldworkers while in Detroit.

Evaluation of Orientation

The first question is whether one week was sufficient
time for orientation. To accomplish some aims, such as the
presentation of goals and research design, operation of the
tape recorder during an interview, and familiarity with the
questionnaire, it would appear that one week was indeed
adequate. For the phonetic drills and the attainment of
an adequate interview technique, however, more time (perhaps
another week) might have been preferable. Sufficient
phonetic drill is imperative. One might have assumed that
fieldworkers had an adequate background in phonetic transcription so that minimal drill was required; however, it was
essential that consistent perception of differences anticipated
in varieties of Detroit speech be attained. More time on
phonetic drills might have more adequately attained this goal.

As for the practice interviews, extending the orientation
period would have allowed more combinations of sex, age, and
race variables to be represented. A desired sample of interviews appropriate to the research design might have been two
children, representing both sexes and one of which was Negro,
one teenager of either sex and any race, two parents, representing both sexes and one of which was Negro, and one grand-
parent of either sex and any race. As it stood, a fieldworker
might, for example, interview his first 10-12 year old Negro
girl in the actual research having interviewed neither a 10-12
year old girl nor a Negro child of either sex during the sample interviews. (The fact that some fieldworkers did not
interview certain types of informants in the sample interviews was compensated for by listening to interviews that
others conducted with a particular informant type during

the interview evaluation.) Another advantage of more practice interviews would have been a more adequate assessment of fieldworker abilities with the different types of informants.

The location of the practice interviews in the Lansing area rather than in Detroit must also be brought into review. Ideally, no one can dispute the fact that practice interviews in Detroit would have been preferable. Unfortunately, there were restrictions of time, budget, and convenience which eliminated this preferable alternative.

Another matter deserving review is the adoption of a standardized phonetic notation system during the course of the orientation week. That a standardized system of phonetic notation is required for a group of eleven fieldworkers can hardly be disputed, but when and how one is to arrive at such a standardization is a matter open to discussion. The adoption of a notation system took place during the latter part of the orientation week, the system being selected by a consensus of the fieldworkers. The advantage of adopting a system during the course of the orientation program lies in the fact that a system could be adopted which would be both maximally useful for transcribing the expected range of sounds in Detroit speech, and also at the same time represent a convenient compromise between the divergent notation systems of the individual fieldworkers. The disadvantage lies in the fact that minimal time is allowed for the adaptation of the fieldworker's personal system, so that he can comfortably transcribe in the standardized system.

A final matter for review is the presentation of desired items in the Short Response section of the questionnaire. Although each item, with a proposed definition for the elicitation of the item, was discussed in orientation, during the actual research it was discovered that several items, especially lexical ones, were misinterpreted by fieldworkers.

For example, the question "What do you call a dish of fruit?"
was designed to elicit the Great Lakes northern variant,
"sauce"; many fieldworkers believed the anticipated response
was "fruit cocktail." Such oversights could only be eliminated by repeated review of the questionnaire and thorough
evaluation of the tape-recorded sample interviews.

5: THE QUESTIONNAIRE

In constructing the questionnaire, the Detroit Dialect Study first investigated questionnaires that had been used by other linguists, most importantly those of the Linguistic Atlas of the United States and Canada; of Raven I. McDavid, Jr.;[3] Lee Pederson and others in Chicago;[4] and of William Labov in New York.[5] An eclectic approach was adopted, for several reasons. First, the fieldworkers were expected to elicit as many styles of speech as possible from the informants, both the single-response style of the Atlas interview and the congeries of styles elicited by Labov's questionnaire: careful speech, casual speech, reading and lists. Moreover, given the stringent time limitations of the interview, it was desirable to collect as much information on each informant's speech as could be gathered in a short time. Finally, where the questions on the Detroit questionnaire are similar or identical to those on earlier questionnaires, it is often because of the potential correlation of Detroit data with that already collected in Chicago and New York. For example,

---

[3] Raven I. McDavid, Jr. and William M. Austin, "Communication Barriers to the Culturally Deprived," U.S.O.E. Cooperative Research Project 2107.

[4] Lee Pederson, The Pronunciation of English in Metropolitan Chicago: Vowels and Consonants, University of Chicago, Ph.D. dissertation, 1964.

[5] William Labov, The Social Stratification of English in New York City, Washington, D.C.: Center for Applied Linguistics, 1966.

the reading passages used in New York were adopted intact
in the expectation that a close comparative analysis would
be made of reading style and phonology in Detroit and New
York. (For the complete text of the Detroit Dialect Study
Questionnaire, see pages 45-57.)

In order to obtain comparable data from children and
adults of different social strata, the questionnaire was
constructed in such a way that only minor adjustments
were necessary to accommodate various age, ethnic and social
groups. The first question of the interview illustrates age
adjustment: the fieldworker asked either, "What kinds of
games do you play around here?" or, "What kinds of games
did you play when you were a kid?" or "What kinds of games
do the kids play around here?" Ethnic adjustments, for
example, were made in eliciting various items which were
found in a delicatessen. Fieldworker adjustments to social
strata were made by de-emphasizing the attention paid to
group fighting when interviewing upper middle class informants.
The object of this standardization was to insure maximum
comparability of the data, so that the differences observed
could properly be ascribed to the important factors of age,
sex, race, and social class. Some independent variables did
of course persist, such as individual informants' interviewing
styles; but the informality of the interview minimized the
former problem, and the structure of the fieldwork team--
living together, interviewing often within hearing of each
other, comparing notes--minimized the latter.

The informality of the interview was a crucial factor
in obtaining data on casual speech in the interview context.
The questionnaire was designed around this central requirement; in fact, the shortcomings of the questionnaire can most
accurately be divided into two main groups: those places where
the informality of the interview was unwittingly violated

(e.g., a few questions about school that were designed to elicit one-word answers included among the discussion questions), and those places where some other goal (e.g., completion of the questionnaire) was sacrificed to maintain the informality.

The framework of the interview was simple and standardized. The fieldworker would hook up the microphone around the informant's neck, start the tape, which had already been threaded onto the machine, and ask the informant to give his name and count to ten. This gave a recited list, one of the more formal styles we wished to obtain, and served as a further identification on the tape in case it should be mixed up with others. The fieldworker would then proceed with Parts I through IV of the questionnaire. On completion of this section of the interview, he would turn the tape over, meanwhile telling the informant the ground rules for Part V. He might say, "Now, what I'm going to do next is try to get you to say some words, but it's cheating if I say them first," and explain that if the informant does not happen to have such a word in his vocabulary that he should just say so, that there are no wrong answers. Most informants could accept this, and could treat the Short Response section as a sort of password game. Then the fieldworker would complete the Informant Data Sheet and begin the Short Response section and Reading section. Finally, time permitting the fieldworker would ask the informant if he had any questions. This was done to obtain question intonation and syntax.

In general, the questionnaire yielded a great deal of discourse and could be completed within the time limitation. (For a sample interview, see Chapter 6.) The one-and-a-half-hour limit was imposed for several reasons: (1) The Uher tape recorder could hold only 5-in. reels, which, when run at 3.75 ips, last for one and a half hours; (2) urban

informants rarely have more time than that to give to the
interviewer; (3) the Study could not possibly have completed
so large a sample if the interviews had been longer. The
questionnaire provided sufficiently diversified topics so
that at least one section might be expected to interest the
informant enough to inspire discourse.

Three different kinds of criticism may be made of the
questionnaire.

First, a number of one-word responses were elicited in
the section primarily intended for the elicitation of discourse. Although the elicitation of single items obtains
more casual responses, it distracts from the elicitation
of spontaneous discourse, the main purpose of the section.
Specifically, it might have been preferable to include
A 1-4 and B of Section II, all of Section III, and B 2
and F 3 of Section IV in the Short Response section.

Secondly, the sections on the informant's occupation
(Section III, D), birthplace and travel (Section III, E 5-8)
might better have been included on the Informant Data Sheet,
even though the travel section occasionally produced an
interesting narrative.

Third, certain questions were either misunderstood
or unproductive for eliciting discourse: Section I, D, and
Section II, E and F. In the latter, because the word "class"
was used, and the questions were asked in a school context,
the informant's answer was occasionally biased toward regarding
intelligence as good scholarship rather than as cunning or
leadership.

Usually, Section I, dealing with games and leisure,
sufficed to initiate narrative; very few informants failed
to respond to at least one of these questions. Almost
everyone had either a most-loved or most-hated teacher to
discuss in Section II. The questions on friendships,

ambitions, holidays, and fighting were reasonably productive; most informants would talk about at least one of them. And the last section, dealing with accidents, close brushes with death, and fate, while not always appropriate for children, drew strong emotional responses from many adults. There was ample material to start all but the most hostile or reticent informants talking. In general, the fieldworkers felt that the discussion questions were more than enough to start the informant talking, and the fieldworkers usually felt free to follow up any line of questioning that seemed productive for the elicitation of discourse.

The Informant Data Sheet might have included additional material useful in stratifying, classifying and otherwise processing the sample. Some of the information needed by the analysts--informant's birthplace, informant's occupation-- was elicited elsewhere in the interview. On the other hand, where the use of a scale for social stratification made it necessary to know how many years of schooling the head of household had received, the analysts were later obliged to contact families in which the wife had been the informant, since this scale for social stratification requires knowledge of the educational achievement, occupation, and residential level of the head of each household. Residential information proved difficult to obtain, as there were no data on Detroit comparable to the ecological studies of other cities in previous sociological research. Consequently, the 1960 U. S. Census block data were used to establish a housing and area scale. (This suggests that in future projects of this sort fieldworkers might be trained to apply housing and residential area scales after each interview.) It might also be suggested that to each data sheet be added the name of the school attended by the base child in each family in order to expedite the organization of the data.

The Short Response section had several items that were
either totally unfamiliar to the informants (the strip between
the sidewalk and the curb) or very difficult to elicit (certain
food and flower terms). But in general the items could be
elicited fairly easily. One problem, the tendency of some older
people to garrulity, could be handled by beginning with
the Short Response section whenever the informant seemed to
be extremely loquacious; otherwise the fieldworker risked
running out of tape with half the short answers left to
elicit. Such problems, however, were rare.

Finally, the Reading Section caused several problems.
It was placed at the end for two reasons: (1) it was poten-
tially the most intimidating section of the interview, and
(2) sequentially it fit into the progression of styles from
less formal to more formal. However, the use of two different
reading passages resulted in problems of comparability. For
example, bright children were often given the longer reading,
while semi-literate adults were given the short diagnostic
list of sentences. It is therefore difficult for anyone
to compare all the children, or all the adults, with each
other. The reading had to be handled diplomatically in
many cases. Perhaps by giving the short reading first,
and then the longer reading to those who did well on the
first, greater comparability could have been achieved.

DETROIT DIALECT STUDY

QUESTIONNAIRE

I. GAMES AND LEISURE   (10 minutes)

A. What kinds of games do you play around here? (perhaps
    marbles, Red Rover, Kick-the-Can, May-I, Capture the
    Flag, Hide and Seek, game with bottle caps)

    1. Note each game and ask about how each is played,
        number of players, etc.

    2. Get terms for "goal," "home," "when a new person
        comes," "getting in free," how you decide who
        is IT, use of rhymes. (also get marbles, jacks,
        hop-scotch, jump rope, tackle-tackle, pom pom,
        roof tag)

B. What are your favorite TV programs? (theaters, movies)
    (elicit recent episode on Batman, UNCLE, etc.)

C. Do you have a pet? Tell me about it.

D. Is there any way you can get a wish? (elicit eye
    lashes, chicken bone, or tooth comes out)

II. SCHOOL (10 minutes)

A. Tell me about your school? What do you study? (get
    geography, history, arithmetic, etc.)

    1. From your seat in class, tell me what you can see.
        (get blackboard, desk, chair)

    2. If you walk outside the classroom, where **are** you?
        (hall) What's in it? (fountain, lockers, stairs)

    3. What's outside the school? (playground, horse,
        swings, teeter totter, monkey bars [define])

    4. What do kids do after school is out? (from
        Negroes, get rippin' and runnin')

B. Did you ever have a teacher who hollered a lot? What
    about?

Did you ever get yelled at? Was it your fault?

C. Can you tell me about the best teacher you ever had? Who was she? Why did you like her?

D. Did you ever have a teacher you just couldn't stand? What was there about her that you didn't like? Did the kids in your class really "trick" your teacher last year?

E. Who was the smartest kid in your class? What did he do that was so good? What favors or rewards does the smart kid get?

F. Who was the dumbest kid? What did he do that was dumb? What does the teacher do to dumb kids?

G. What time do you get out of school? (or, What time does it start?) (get quarter till, of, to_____)

III. GROUP STRUCTURE (10 minutes)

A. For child: Is there a bunch of guys you always hang around with and do stuff with?

   For adult: Is there a group of people you used to (associate) with?

   1. About how old are they? (Were/are they about the same age?)

   2. Child: And you're_____(how old)?
      Adult: Are they still the same ones? Do you still see them a lot? If not, who?

   3. Do any of the guys (people) speak Polish? Spanish? Hungarian, etc.?

   4. Are there any Negro (white, Jewish) kids (people) in your bunch (group)?

B. In your bunch (group), is there one guy(person) that everybody listens to (regards as leader)?

   1. Why? (smartest, biggest, etc.)

   2. Can new kids get into your bunch? How?

C. What do you want to be when you finish school?
    (What did you hope to be when you were younger?)
    How long does it take to become a_____?
    What does a _____do?
    If you could do it all over again, what would you
    want to be?
    If you had all the money you could ever want, all
    the money in the world, what would you do with it?

D. Your job (for men or working women). Describe
    what you do in a day's work. (try to get specialized
    vocabulary of the occupation)
    Where do you work?_____

E. Neighborhood
    1. What do they call this part of town?_____
    2. What are the boundaries?_____
    3. What is this city called?_____(if
        necessary by now).
    4. What are some streets of Detroit? What about
        the big ones?
        a. The one that goes to East Detroit? (Gratiot)
        b. The one that goes by the University of Detroit?
            (Livernois)
        c. Down by Cobo Hall is_____? (Fort Street)
        d. The one that Hudson's is on? (Woodward) (get
            others, too) Get expressways or freeways,
            too (Ford, Lodge, Chrysler)
    5. Where were you born?_____
    6. Where else have you lived in Detroit?
    7. Where else have you lived outside of Detroit?
    8. Where have you gone on trips?

F. Special Occasions
    1. How does your family celebrate the holidays?

(for Jewish kids--Bar Mitzvah; for Jewish girls--
Baz Mitzvah) (Catholics--first communion)
(elicit family or group customs and terms, especially religious elements, special cooking, gifts,
etc.)

2. What would you like for Christmas this year? (if
   a bike, etc., describe it)
   What was the best Christmas present you ever
   got? (Jewish holiday--Hanukkah)

3. What do you do on October 31? (elicit pumpkins,
   Halloween, witch)
   a. When you ring the doorbell, what do you say?
   b. Tell me about your costume last year. If
      you had your choice, what would you choose
      this year?

IV. FIGHTING, ACCIDENTS AND ILLNESS (10 minutes)
   A. What kinds of things do fights usually start about
      around here?
      1. Are there rules for a fair fight? (When is it
         over? Does the loser say "uncle", "I give"?)
         (IF you get nothing above)
         If you saw someone kicking someone else on the
         ground (or using a stick, or a chain, or a
         lead pipe, etc.) and it was supposed to be
         a fair fight, what would you do?
      2. Did you ever see anyone get beat up real bad?
         What happened to him?
      3. Did you ever get into a fight with a guy bigger
         than you? What happened?
      4. Do the guys usually fight one-against-one or in
         gangs? What are the rules for gang fights?
   B. Have you ever been in the hospital?

1. What is the worst illness you have ever had?
   Describe it (and others).

2. When a person starts to sneeze or cough, you
   might say he is _____(catching, taking)
   a cold.

C. Have you ever been in an automobile accident?
   (or, Tell me the worst one you ever saw--draw out
   details).

D. Were you ever in a situation where you thought
   you might be killed or die?
   After response, ask: Sometimes people say
   whatever is going to happen is going to happen.
   How do you feel about that?

V. SHORT RESPONSE

A. In and About the House
    1. living room (front room, parlor, sitting room)
    2. dining room
    3. kitchen (breakfast room, nook, summer kitchen)
    4. bathroom (john, lavatory)
    5. bedroom
    6. hall (foyer, vestibule)
    7. closet (also: movable closet, wardrobe)
    8. attic (garret, loft)
    9. basement (cellar)
    10. roof
    11. chimney
    12. soot
    13. gutters (eavestroughs, spouting)

B. Other Buildings and Features
    1. garage
    2. outhouse (privy)
    3. shed
    4. patio (describe)

    5. porch (stoop)--with or without roof

    6. grass strip between sidewalk and curb

    7. barn

    8. creek

C. <u>Furniture</u>

  <u>In Bedroom</u>:

    1. bed

    2. dresser (define--with mirror)

    3. chest of drawers

    4. wardrobe

    5. cover for bed (comfort, comforter)

  <u>In Living Room</u>:

    6. couch (sofa, davenport)

    7. chairs

  <u>In Kitchen</u>:

    8. table

    9. refrigerator (fridge, icebox)

  10. stove (range)

  <u>In Other Rooms</u>:

D. <u>Foods and Cooking</u>

  What do you call the morning meal?_____

  What do you eat then?

    1. eggs

    2. doughnuts (fried cakes)

    3. pancakes (flapjacks)

    4. coffee (how do you prepare it? cook? make? boil?

    5. sausage (links, little pigs)

    6. bacon (sidemeat, salt pork)

    7. hogs

    8. syrup

    9. waffles

  10. toast

11. milk

12. jelly

What do you call the noon meal?_____

What do you eat then?

1. cottage cheese (smearcase, Dutch cheese, pot cheese)

2. hamburger (hamburg) (What is on it when it has everything?)

   onions

   mustard

   catsup

   mayonnaise

3. sandwich designed to be a meal (submarine, hero, grinder, poor boy, hoagie)

4. hot dogs (franks, wieners, wienies)

5. What do they sell at a delicatessen?

What do you call the evening meal?_____

What do you have?

1. meats (special cuts of beef or steak)

2. potatoes (white and sweet) (potato chips)

3. green beans (snap beans, string beans, etc.)

4. greens (collard, turnip, dandelion, mustard)

5. corn-on-the-cob (roasting ears, sweet corn)

6. lima beans (butter beans)

7. peas (black-eyed, English)

8. carrots

9. vegetables

What goes into a salad?

1. lettuce

2. celery

3. cabbage

4. radishes

5. tomato

What desserts do you eat?

1. ice cream

2. cookies (cake, pie)

3. dish of fruit (sauce?)

4. melons (muskmelon)

5. fruits (center of peach, center of cherry)

Between Meals

1. snack (bite, lunch)

2. carbonated drink (pop, soda)

3. rootbeer float (Boston Cooler, Black Cow)
    (note variations)

Nuts

4. pecan

5. cashew

6. peanuts

7. Brazil nut (nigger toe)

8. almond

E. Household Terms

1. frying pan (skillet, spider--also electric)

2. spoon

3. spatula (kid cheater, scraper)

4. apron

5. greasy

6. washing

7. iron

8. straightens up (redds up)

9. washes

10. rinses

11. dries (wipes)

12. bucket (pail)

13. faucet

14. (paper) sack (bag)

F. <u>Miscellaneous</u>

   1. babies (creep, crawl)

   2. baby buggy (cab, carriage)

   3. sick to (on, at) your stomach

   4. zinnias

   5. portulaca (Fourth of July)

   6. peony

   7. letter carrier

   8. cop

   9. guarantee

  10. armful (armload)

  11. chipmunk (ground squirrel)

  12. Battle Creek

  13. mantel/mantelpiece

  14. hearth

  15. toilet

  16. sink

  17. bathtub

  18. (medicine)_____

  19. kitchen cupboard/cabinet

  20. catch (take) cold

  21. quarter (to, till, of, before) five

<u>READING</u>

one	six	Tuesday
two	seven	Wednesday
three	eight	Thursday
four	nine	Friday
five	ten	Saturday
		Sunday
		Monday

Last month I read five books.

Tom read all the time.

So... I sold my soul to the devil.

When I passed by, I read the posters.

Don't you dare hit your dear little brother.

When I liked a story, I read every word.

They cost a nickel yesterday, but today they cost a dime.

Now I read and write better than Alfred does.

I looked for trouble when I read the news.

"NOBODY KNOWS YOUR NAME"

Last year I went out for the basketball team, and I
made out better than I expected. I wasn't too big, but I
was quick on my feet, and my jump shot used to drop in when
it counted. The coach told me himself I was a real help to
the school.

But you couldn't tell that to Eleanor. No matter if I
did good or bad, she'd ask me after every game: "Why can't
you be the man to put it in the basket?" I'd tell her, "Look,
Eleanor, everybody can't be a star. I'm not a forward; I'm
not a center; I'm a guard. I play the back court."

"But you passed it to Lester again," she used to say,
"you must have passed it to Lester sixty times, and he
missed it most of the time. Why don't you make the shots?"
"It's easy enough to explain," I told her, "if you only know
what's what. Lester is seven-foot-two; I'm five-foot-ten.
He just twists his wrist and puts it in."

She wouldn't see it, and I couldn't make her see it.
I'd talk till I was out of breath, but I might as well have
kept my mouth shut. It was always something: if it wasn't
this thing, it was that thing, or the other thing. I'd tell
her again, "Look Eleanor, I'm a guard. I play the back court."

Then she tried a new line. "I know you're right," she
said. "But what about my pride? I don't think any of my

friends remember if you're a center or an end or a tackle. Nobody knows your name!"

She made my blood boil. I said I wasn't going to hog the ball to please her. I was ready for murder or worse. And she said she wouldn't go out with me any more if I didn't score a lot of points. So I told the coach about it. He said, "Artie, everybody can't be a star. You're a good team man. It should be an easy game tomorrow night, so we'll keep setting you up."

They fixed me up to look good all right. I just hung under the basket, and everybody passed me the ball. I pushed the easy ones in, and nobody noticed when I missed. By the end of the game, I had thrown in thirty-three points. The whole school was cheering for me: Everybody was shouting my name.

Everybody that is, but Eleanor. I looked for her here, there, everywhere--but there wasn't hide nor hair of her. Finally I called her father on the phone. "I just made thirty-three points, Mr. Jones--but I can't find Eleanor. Do you know where she is?"

Her father said, "Just a minute." Then he said, "She says she can't come to the phone right now, son. She's watching the Dave Clark Five on Channel 2. But she says, will you please do it for her again next week--she can watch you then."

Next year I'm going out for the swimming team--under water. Down there, nobody--but nobody--is going to know my name.

INFORMANT DATA SHEET

Name_____Sex_____Age_____

Address_____Race_____

Highest grade level reached in school_____

Schools attended_____

_____

Oldest child in family?   Yes   No

If not oldest, what?_____

Parents birthplace:

                                   Grandfather_____
        Father_____
                                   Grandmother_____

                                   Grandfather_____
        Mother_____
                                   Grandmother_____

Religion (be as specific as possible)_____

What language besides English is spoken?_____

                    At home?_____

Father's occupation_____

Mother's occupation_____

Spouse's occupation_____

Spouse's birthplace_____

Other places spouse has lived_____

_____

Nationality_____

Birthplace_____

Other places lived_____

_____

Years in Detroit_____

Spouse's parents birthplace: Father_____

                                          Mother_____

Maiden Name_____

Friends (Detroit and others)_____

_____

_____

_____

_____

6: FIELDWORK

Upon completion of their daily interviews, the fieldworkers were responsible for transcribing phonetically Section V of each interview. A sample page of such phonetic transcription is shown in Fig. 10.

After the fieldworkers had phonetically transcribed Section V of every interview, these transcriptions were recoded into alpha-numeric symbols which were keypunched and verified for a computer retrieval program. The program was geared for retrieval of both phonological and lexical items. In order to do this, it was necessary to devise a code book in which all informant background data and lexical variants could be coded.

The Code Book

The code book included separate fields for each salient bit of information required of each informant. Field number 1 for example, was for tape number, field 2 for informant's name, field 3 for sex, etc. In all, 34 fields were devoted to informant background data.

Language data fields began at field 35 and extended through field 170. Fig. 11 is a sample page from the code book.

The code book specifies that any phonetic transcription of field 35, for example, must be for one of the four subcategories of that field (living room, parlor, sitting room, front room). Thus ['pʰarlɪr] would be coded under 35.2. Every field had an open number of subcategories so that, as the coding proceeded

V. Lexical

A. IN AND ABOUT THE HOUSE

1. living room (<u>front</u> room, parlor, sitting room)

2. <u>dining</u> room

3. <u>kitchen</u> (breakfast room, nook, summer kitchen)

4. bathroom

5. <u>bedroom</u>

6. <u>hall</u> (foyer, vestibule)

7. <u>closet</u> (movable closet-wardrobe)

8. <u>attic</u> (garret, loft)

9. <u>basement</u> (cellar)

10. <u>roof</u>

11. chimney

12. soot

13. <u>gutters</u> (eavestroughs, spouting)

Fig. 10. Sample of Phonetic Transcription

35. Living Room
    1. living room
    2. parlor
    3. sitting room
    4. front room
36. Dining Room
    1. dining room
37. Kitchen
    1. kitchen
38. Bathroom
    1. bathroom
    2. john
    3. lavatory
    4. powder room
39. Bedroom
    1. bedroom
    2. chamber
    3. chamber room
40. Hall
    1. hall
    2. hallway
    3. vestibule
    4. entrance way
    5. entrance hall
    6. main hall
    7. corridor

41. Closet
    1. closet
42. Attic
    1. attic
    2. loft
    3. garrett
43. Basement
    1. basement
    2. cellar
44. Roof
    1. roof
45. Chimney
    1. chimney
    2. smoke stack
46. Soot
    1. soot
    2. coal dust
47. Gutters
    1. gutters
    2. eavestroughs
    3. spouting
48. Other
    1. breakfast nook

Fig. 11.   Sample Page from Code Book

lexical responses noted for the first time could be added.
This flexibility was particularly useful in the more general
fields,   e.g., field 100, in which almost 100 various
meats eaten for dinner were recorded. Furthermore, at the
end of each broad lexical area, e.g., names for furniture,

a separate field was assigned for volunteered responses which, though in the general semantic area, were not specifically requested by the fieldworker. Consequently almost any response could have been coded from the phonetic transcriptions but once it was assigned a number within a field, no other lexical variant could be classed with it.

To be sure, the coders frequently had to make decisions on borderline matters. For example, corn-on-the-cob (106.1) was occasionally recorded as corn-on-the-carp, corn-on-the-car and corn-on-the-horn, as opposed to the more usual variants, roasting ears and sweet corn. In such cases, the coders categorized by the more normative variants and corn-on-the-carp was coded under corn-on-the-cob.

Coding

Two assistants coded all the phonetic transcriptions of Section V of the interview, using the symbols shown in Figs. 12-14.

The data were transferred from questionnaire sheets to punched card coding forms as follows: From left to right on the card, material is punched, one character per column, and when there is too much for one card, coding carries over from column 72 to column 1 of the next card. Each field is coded consecutively starting with the first and ending with one blank field after the last one on the questionnaire. The field number is punched, followed by a period (.) followed by each coded subfield for that field. A subfield is coded by first punching its lexical code, followed by a left parenthesis, followed by encipherment of each phonetic symbol according to the phonetic coding scheme. After all the phonetic symbols are coded, the subfield is terminated by a right parenthesis. Each additional subfield is coded immediately afterwards in exactly the same way, and after the last right parenthesis

b	B		ł	L-		t	T
č	C		m	M		č̌	T(
d	D		n	N		ď	D(
ð	D-		ŋ	NX		tʰ	TH
f	F		p	P		čʰ	CH
g	G		pʰ	PH		θ	T-
h	H		ʔ	Q		v	V
ǰ	J		r	R		z	Z
k	K		r̃	R$		ž	Z(
kʰ	KH		r̥̃	R-		w	W
l	L		R̥̃	RX$		y	Y
l,	LX		s	S		x	KS
			š	S(			

Fig. 12. Consonant Code Sheet

of the last subfield is a slash (/). The next field is
coded the same way, and each blank field appears on the
record as a field number followed by a period and a slash.

A sample of the coded material is as follows:

37.1   (∅KHU2C*U7*N)/ for [kʰɪč<ɪn] (kitchen)

39.1   (∅BU417DRU1014U7$EM)/ for [be·drᵿᵎm] (bedroom)

The Computer Program[6]

To facilitate the display of the correlation of such non-
linguistic factors as age, status, sex, race and geographical
origins, it was decided that a distribution table, or a
"contingency table," would be convenient. A contingency table
of one variable versus another variable with respect to a
particular population is a tabulation of the number of people
who fall into the categories defined by all possible combination

---

[6] The authors are indebted to Edward N. Adams for devising
the computer program in this study.

i	U1		ə	U8
ɪ	U2		ɑ	U9
e	U3		u	U10
ɛ	U4		ʊ	U11
æ	U5		o	U12
a	U6		ɔ	U13
ɨ	U7		ɒ	U14

Glides   E

For example: [aⁱ] U6U1E

[ⁱu] EU1U10

Fig. 13.   Vowel Code Sheet

V∧	raised	I1	?	coarticulation	?+
Vᵛ	lowered	I2	C	retroflexed	$
Ṽ	nasalized	I3	C	syllabic	A
V̨	weakly nasalized	I4	¬	unreleased	+
V	rounded ↔ unrounded	I5	C	devoiced	,
V	slightly rounded	I6	C<	fronted	*
V·	length	I7	C>	backed	$
V:	extra length	I8	C	voiced → devoiced	=
V́	laryngealized	I9	C	voiceless → voiced	'
V	pharyngealized	I10	C	lenis	8/5
V+	breathy	I11	'	stress	Ø

Fig. 14.   Modifications

of the two variables. The program is devised to accommodate the following general tasks:

(1) To maintain a large permanent file of answers for all the respondents;

(2) To provide a convenient means for the linguist to specify hypotheses as to the relevant categorization of any given variable;

(3) To assess the information file by requesting
     contingency tables of several variables so
     categorized with each other.

After the file of information was punched on computer
cards, it was stored permanently on magnetic tapes in a
machine-oriented form. Two copies of the permanent tape were
made. One of these is used by the linguist as the permanent
tape, to produce a recoded tape for use in making tables.
The second serves as a back-up tape in case of loss or
deterioration of the other.

The program reads the cards and puts the information in
slightly different form onto tape. If the reading program
encounters two contiguous fields whose numbers are not in
order and consecutive, then the whole record for that respondent is rejected with instructions to correct the cards and
put them back in. Thus it is also true that if a record
does not begin with the word PERSON, then the program will
reject that respondent's cards.

The second program is the part which enables the
linguist to temporarily recode the permanent data into a few
categories according to phonological criteria and to give
these categories mnemonic names. These names will ultimately
be used by the third program as row and column headings.
The linguist will have prepared a deck of recode packs, and
the program will read all of them. Then it starts reading
the permanent tape, one person at a time. After it has
read the information for one person, it looks at the first
recode pack, and finds out which field number it refers to.
Then it skips to that place on the person's record, tries
to scan this field for the first set of characteristics, and
keeps going until it finds a set of characteristics which
this field satisfies. Next it writes on the temporary tape
the category name associated with that set. It then looks

at the next recode pack, and goes through this routine again,
until all the recode packs have been treated for this speaker,
and all of the categories have been written on tape for this
person. Then the next person is read in from the permanent
tape, and he is treated in the same way. When the entire
permanent tape has been treated, this program is finished,
and the next program can then be used.

The next program merely sets up tables on the basis of
table requests supplied by the linguist in the following
form: V1xV2xV3, which will produce a table in which variable
V1 appears spread down the side, V2 spread across the top
and V3 spread in each cell of the table. Each row will have
heading, which is one category name. Each column will
similarly have a heading and at the intersection of a row
and a column will be a list of all the third variable
headings with numbers following them indicating the number
of people answering that combination of three.

The following is illustrative of the kind of display
available in this program:

VOWEL OF "fog"	10-12 year-olds	teenagers	parents
[ɑ] [ɑ^] [ɑ<]	211	150	130
[ɔ] [ɔ<] [ɒ]	23	25	94
[oᵘ] [ɔ^ᵘ] [oᵛᵘ]	10	23	27

Interview Typescripting

As the interviews were completed, certain tapes were
selected for typescripting by staff secretaries. Sections
I-IV were typescripted in normal English orthography
to provide a convenient reference base for future grammatical and phonological analysis. In typescripting it was
found necessary to include the fieldworkers' questions as
well as the informants' responses. Unless the fieldworkers'
questions were included, the discourse appeared disconnected
and grammatical analysis was particularly difficult.

This technique has been subsequently shown to be useful as a preliminary keying device in William K. Riley's research on English nasal consonants.[7] Riley marked the typescripts at places where nasal consonants might be expected to occur. Then he carefully listened to the tapes, transcribing the nasal consonants along with the environments which interested him.

The usefulness of the typescript for grammatical analysis is even more apparent. The analytical procedures outlined in the final report of the Detroit Dialect Study to the U.S. Office of Education demonstrate this usefulness.[8] Following are examples of two somewhat different kinds of interviews. The first, No. 230, is an example of an interview in which the questionnaire was pursued rather thoroughly. The second, No. 241, illustrates the type of interview in which the fieldworker, sensing the informant's natural tendency and willingness to talk, allows the conversation to go where it will. Many of the interview questions were never asked.

The latter type of interview is, from the analyst's point of view, superior to the former, which seems slightly less natural. But not all informants are inherently talkative and the questionnaire is intended to bring out as much conversation as possible.

---

[7] William K. Riley, Socially Determined Variation In The Nasal Consonants of English, unpublished M.A. thesis, Michigan State University, 1967.

[8] Roger W. Shuy, Walter A. Wolfram and William K. Riley, Linguistic Correlates of Social Stratification in Detroit Speech, Final Report, Cooperative Research Project 6-1347, U.S. Office of Education, 1967.

Interview No. 230

FIELDWORKER: What kind of games did you play when you were
               younger?

INFORMANT: Tag, shoe mate, hide and go seek.

FW: How do you play tag?

IN: We (chase) we chase each other.

FW: How about hide and go seek, how did you play it?

IN: Uhm, we put our foot in and the last person who out
      they go and hide their eyes go and hide their eyes
      and we go and hide and they try to find us.

FW: And what did you say when you put your feet in, any
      rhyme that you use?

IN: "I struck the match and it went out," and "engine,
      engine, number nine, going down Chicago line, if the
      train jump the track, would you want your money back?"

FW: Good, any more?

IN: One potato...uhm "my mother, your mother live across
      the street, 1490 Alligator Street, every night they
      had a fight and this is what they say, ackabacker
      soda cracker, ackabacka boo, ackabacker soda cracker,
      and out go you."

FW: Hey good, any more. Hey, this is neat.

IN: Can't think of no more.

FW: Good. How about any other game you can think of.
      How about hopscotch?

IN: We played that.

FW: I don't know how to play that. I'm a boy, tell me
      how to play it.

IN: Well you draw a line across from each other on the
      sidewalk. And you number them. Then you put your
      rock in then you go from one, you don't step in number
      one 'cause you rock is in, then you go to two, then
      three, then four, then five, six and seven and eight.

Don't jump out, because you be out, and you turn around
and go back. And when you get to number two you pick up
your rock and jump out if somebody else is playing. And
you go to number two, three, and four and the rest of them
the same way.

FW: Good, how about any other games, any other games you can
think of? How about Red Rover?

IN: I don't know how to play that.

FW: Marbles?

IN: Yeah, I know how to play marbles.

FW: How do you play that? Tell me how you play that?

IN: Well we play chase and one...the first person they throw
their marble in and then the other person try to hit
them. Then if you get right close up to them and then
you miss them, you can say "blocksy" and you block
them and if they miss you, well then you get a chance to
hit them.

FW: Good what are your favorite TV programs?

IN: Uhm Honey West and...

FW: Did you see Honey West last week? Can you tell me
about it? Tell me all everything that you can remember.

IN: Uh, Honey West. Well Honey West just got through taking
care of this little girl and she said she was going to
get a water they in the uh, in the airport. And then
they went over there, this man change bag with that little
girl and they didn't see him. So the little girl went over
there to get some water and then Honey West and them went
over there and they...she wasn't there. So, she uhm,
they was looking for her. So Honey West went back to the
office and they had found out they had the wrong bag,
so they had pour, pour all the uhm things that was out
in the other bag was shaving things, and 'lectric shaver
and a shaving brush and a cup and all like that. And uhm,

uhm uh, Honey West tiger, Bruce, he was playing with the
thing and knocked the shaving brush over and it came open
and it was whole lots of diamonds and rubies and emeralds
in it. And they said they the person was smuggling it.
So the person came there, the man who had change bag
came there with the little girl wanted his bag. So Honey
West helper, he went to get the bag and uhm, the little
girl went over there and got the bag, she said, first
she had to give him the bag before they could trade,
you know, each other. So they went there, she gave him
the bag. She gave the little girl the bag and she gave
it to the man and the man let her go and they went.
So, they had gone...Honey West had gave him a pen it had
a Geiger counter in it and, you know, they follow it.
And well they went and they was following him in the
truck they had and uhm, they lost it 'cause he had broke
the pen after he had got to the hotel downtown, it was
lost downtown. So when they got back to the office they
was uh mess up, all tore up and everything and tiger
was tore up, you know. They had wrapped him up in
something. That was all. So they had got in touch
wit the thing again. So well finally they got where
uh the little pen was signaling something and it was
their auntie and a little girl. So then one day the
man, another man coming in there about he needed their
help and he told Honey West where to meet him, one
that night. So they went there that night, Honey West
did and uhm, her partner he follow her and uhm they
had trapped Honey West and they had tied her and her
and this other man was in there they was watching
Honey West, so he was talking about he a headache and
she rolled in and start rubbing his shoulder and then
all of sudden she did like that and he was knocked out.

So then another man came outside and he attached uh
Honey West partner and he gave him a judo chop and he
was knocked out. So they broke in there, Honey West's
partner he was he was knocking on the door and one
of the mens came to the door and he said, he opened
the door and the other man came in there and they was
fighting and they had, had them, you know, they're
set to call the police. So another man come in there and
say, "you don't have to do that" and uh so, they went
to give him the bag with the jewel and things in and so
Honey West saw some scratches on the man's hand so she
gave him a judo chop and knocked him out and her partner
ask her "what, what'd he do that for?" so she said, the
scratch is from Bruce Handcock at, at the office when
the office was tore up it was some blood on the sheet
what the man whoever had tied put Bruce in a bag and
that's the end of it.

FW: Good. How about the man from UNCLE, have you ever watched
    him? Did you watch him last week?

IN: They didn't have him on last week.

FW: How about Batman? What are some of your other favorite
    programs?

IN: Uhm.

FW: The Fugitive?

IN: I watch that once in a while. And let's see. TV programs?
    I watch...

FW: A movie.

IN: A movie?

FW: Tell me a movie you saw recently.

IN: Oh I saw the "Creature That Walked Among Us."

FW: Okay, tell me about that.

IN: There was this creature and something like "The Creature
    From The Black Lagoon," and they had went to capture this

creature and they had captured it and took him back to
civilization. So uhm they had operated him on on the
boat that's before they got in, just before they got
back to the, uh United States and they had made his lungs
where he could live above the water. And so the animal,
he had jumped off the boat, and he had got loose and jumped
off and the man jumped in there to save him because, you
know, you can't breath under the water. And so he brought
him back up. So he they has, had to have some kind of
protection on his skin so they put him on men pajamas.
They had, the creature had got off the truck after he
got back to where the man lived and uhm, he uh had put
the animal in a cage and the animal right from the cage
down, there down was some water, you know, it was something to be like a swimming pool but it wasn't exactly,
something like a it was a lake rather. And he didn't
even recognized the water, you know, so there was this
uh tiger and he had...in this other pen besides the
creature was some sheep and this tiger had climbed up
there on the uh tree and jumped in there and was
supposed to eat one of the sheeps and the animal had
broke that uh fence and killed the tiger. He picked him
up and threw him down. So the man say, the creature
didn't like to see other people hurt by something, you
know, and uhm, he uhm, this other man liked this man wife,
you know the man who owned the place and they went for
a swim and then they came out and the man, and the lady
husband saw them. So that night the man that owned the
place made him, went and told that man to move out and
the man asked him "why 'cause his wife" and he said,
"never mind just get out." So he gave him some money
for doing his work and everything and went to leave. And
as they (walked) as they was walking down the stair the

other man he hit that man that was supposed to leave
and the animal saw that. So the man that owned the place
picked up that man and was going to take him in the
creature cage and put him in there, he was dead. So
he went over there and pulled the thing and it opened
then he went and put the man in...it when he went to
lock the thing the creature got real mad, and he (start)
he broke the fence down and he started chasing the man.
He chased him up within the stairs and through the
house and tore up the house real badly. And there was
this lady, she started screaming. Then this other man
came out of there and he went in there and he was holding
on to her and the man had creeped in the hall and knocked
over something and he ran out the door and the creature
turned around and broke the window and picked up the
man and knocked him down then he throw him down. Then
the creature walked down the stairs and uhm, he went
through the through the, uh fence and it was electric,
you know, had barb wires and electric wires on it and he
had walked, and he had walked to a mountainside of a
cliff and he started walking down it was it was the
river and then that was the end of it.

FW: Good. Do you have the...that's good. Your are a good
     story teller. Do you have a pet? A dog or anything?

IN: No.

FW: Would you like to have one?

IN: No.

FW: Any particular pet you would like to have?

IN: Yeah.

FW: What?

IN: A poodle.

FW: Why would you like to have a poodle?

IN: I don't know, I just want one.

FW: Is there any way you can get a wish, say you're eating
    chicken or something, what's that bone in the middle?

IN: We call it a wishing bone.

FW: Uh huh, how does that work?

IN: One person hold the other end and another person hold that
    end, you make a wish and then you break it. Then the
    little piece that's sticking up, whoever has that piece
    their wish suppose to come true.

FW: Uh huh, did you ever do that?

IN: (Yes.)

FW: Did your wish come true?

IN: Once in a while.

FW: If you had a wish now, what would you wish for?

IN: I don't know.

FW: How about when you lose a tooth, when you used to lose
    a tooth when you were younger, what happened?

IN: Well when we was little, when we lose a tooth, we put
    it, we put it uhm under our pillow and my mother said a
    good fairy come and the next morning our tooth be gone
    and we have some money under there.

FW: Oh good. Tell me about your school, what do you study?

IN: Oh English and math and science and homemaking, health.

FW: Uh huh, what is your favorite subject in school and why?

IN: Oh, let's see, homemaking, you learn how to sew and cook
    and learn different things and how to do different things,
    housework.

FW: Uh huh, have you sewed anything?

IN: (Yes.)

FW: What did you sew?

IN: I sewed a apron, but I didn't finish it because they had
    changed my classes my schedule. My schedule is different
    from the other kids.

FW: Good. Tell me from your seat in the class, what can you

see, what are some of the things you can see?

IN: Well I can look out the window, I can see the blackboard, see any, anything in the room.

FW: And what do you sit in ?

IN: We sit at at a (table)... in some our class we sit in a desk, in the other classes, uhm three classes we sit in a desk and the other ones, in gym we (slit) sit on the floor and the other ones we (have) sit at the tables we have table and chairs to sit at.

FW: Uh huh, how many things to sit in the classroom about, have you any idea? How many what, how many tables or desks?

IN: There's (one) there's six uh six tables in uh science and we have...

FW: About how many places are there to sit?

IN: Uhm about, it's only one place.

FW: I mean in the regular rooms where you don't have tables.

IN: We sit in the desks, one behind each other.

FW: How many are there?

IN: Eight.

FW: Eight? About how many are there in the whole room about?

IN: Forty, forty desses.

FW: Uh huh, good. Okay, what do you call this part here?

IN: The rail?

FW: Yeah, it's a a pole?

IN: A pole?

FW: A post?

IN: Post of a bed, I guess.

FW: Yeah, how many does it have, how many does the bed have?

IN: Four.

FW: Four what?

IN: Posts.

FW: Okay good. If you walk outside the classroom, where are you?

IN: In the hall.

FW: And what's in there?

IN: Well it's a water fountain and doors to the other rooms.

FW: Uh huh, good. What's outside the school, say when you
     were grammar school, in elementary school, what was
     outside there?

IN: It was a playground.

FW: And what was some of the things in the playground?

IN: Had swings and sliding boards, and...

FW: Anything you could go up and down a long board you
     could sit on?

IN: Uh a see-saw. They had tires that you can go through
     and climb over.

FW: Good. How about those bars you can climb over.

IN: Monkey bars.

FW: And what are they like? What...

IN: Well lots of bars connected together and you can climb
     all the way up to the top and you can go through them.

FW: Good. What do the kids do after school's out?

IN: They go home and if kids have homework they do their
     homework then go outside and play.

FW: What do you do?

IN: Well I come home and I do my work and I do my homework,
     maybe. And then I go outside and play.

FW: Good. Did you ever have a teacher that hollered a lot?

IN: Yeah, one of my teachers.

FW: About what?

IN: About sitting in my seat.

FW: Uh huh. What are some of the things she hollered about?

IN: Well I be sitting in my seat and she be talking and all she
     did was talk and tell us to do something and we start
     doing it. She start talking again then, then when we
     start doing our work, something she say, you can't

hardly tell what's she's saying, she go so fast. And then
you ask the person uh what she say, and then the next thing
you know you got a three ten pass after school, that's
all.

FW: Is that right. Was it ever your fault when she hollered
at you?

IN: Nope. She make any kind of excuse. One time I dropped
my money on the floor, it was a movie on, and she put
my name on a slip 'cause of that and I had to come after
school.

FW: Uh huh. Can you tell me about the best teacher you ever
had? Who was she?

IN: Well my best teacher was Miss Drake.

FW: What was...why did you like her?

IN: She was nice. When she give us give us work, she give
us work, well the way she give it to us, we could
easily get through with it and be easier to find if
there's something to find in the book. And if you
needed didn't know the answer she, go up there and
ask her, she'd tell you you the right answers. She
don't give you, tell you where to look, she just tell
you the answer.

FW: Uh huh. Did you ever have a teacher you just couldn't
stand?

IN: (Yes.)

FW: Tell me about her.

IN: That's my social study teacher, Miss Barkley. That's
the one that always giving three ten passes.

FW: Uh huh.

IN: Then we say, all she know is three ten passes.

FW: Uh huh. Did the kids in your class ever trick the teacher
this year?

IN: Yes. Lots of time.

FW: Okay tell me a couple of times when you tricked the teacher
    what do you do?

IN: Well one time we wrote "hit me on top of my head" and we
    we put it on a piece of paper then we put a hole through
    it and we put it on her back and she be walking through the
    hall with that on her back. And we put paper in her hair.
    And then one day she bought some new shoes and so "look you
    all Miss Barkley got some new shoes," and we laugh and every-
    thing. And we uhm, uh well, we tell her we want to go some
    place and she give us a pass and we don't come back.

FW: Uh huh, good. How about any other tricks that you pulled
    on the teacher?

IN: Uhm. We had a, some of our friends from another room come
    in there and said the office want us and we get out the
    room.

FW: Good. Who is the smartest kid in your class?

IN: Who the smartest?

FW: Yes.

IN: What's her name?

FW: Yeah.

IN: Martha William.

FW: What does she do that's so good?

IN: Well she get all A's in her work. She, she not the
    talk...talkative like. She don't like to talk a lot. And
    she the quite type, she don't like to be playing all like
    that, she like to work and that's all.

FW: What favors or rewards does a smart kid get from a teacher?

IN: Well, this semester she got uh, a map from the social
    study teacher and she got an honor award from the teacher.
    She made this scholarship in citizenship, perfect atten-
    dance and best girl award and that's all.

FW: Good. Who is the dumbest kid?

IN: That's hard to say, let me see. The dumbest kid in our

room is a boy name Dennis Moore.

FW: What did he do that was dumb?

IN: He never get his work done. He never study his words
our teacher give us and all he did, got E. And it's...
no wonder he didn't fail.

FW: What does the teacher do with dumb kids?

IN: Give them a crack. Make them stay after school.

FW: Good. What time do you get out of school?

IN: Well the real time, it supposed to be in our school is
three thirty. But if you had done all your work and
ain't got to stay after school for no one, you get
out of school at three-o-five.

FW: Say if you get out of school at three thirty and you have
to stay after school fifteen minutes what time would you
get out?

IN: What time would you get out?

FW: Yes. If you had to stay after school fifteen minutes and
you get out at three thirty.

IN: Three forty-five.

FW: Is there any other way you can say that? Quarter...

IN: Quarter after, or quarter to um four?

FW: Yes. Is that what you would say?

IN: Yes.

FW: Quarter...

IN: To four.

FW: Good. Is there a bunch of girls you go around with in
the neighborhood?

IN: Yes once in a while.

FW: Uh huh, and how old are they?

IN: Thirteen and fourteen and fifteen.

FW: Uh huh, tell me about them, what do you do together?

IN: Well we just go walking and that's all. We just walk.

FW: What do you like to talk about, tell me some of the

```
         things you talk about with your friends.
IN:  Well, talk about boys and we talk about girls that
     was our friend.  And girls that was two-faced.  And
     girls who you can't tell nobody nothing without them
     going and telling the person.  And girls we have fights
     with and different things like that.
FW:  Tell me, what type of boy do you like, what is your
     favorite type of boy?
IN:  Hmmm.  Nice, intelligent.  He has to be good-looking too.
FW:  He does.  What's a good-looking boy, tell me a good-
     looking boy.
IN:  I don't, I can't, I can't say.
FW:  You can't.  Does he have to be four feet tall or what?
IN:  Well about five feet five.  Nice brown eyes, good hair.
     Nice smile.
FW:  Good.  Do you have a boy friend now?  What's he like,
     tell me about him?
IN:  He five feet six, he got nice hair, he got brown eyes.
     Nice. He intelligent, give me anything I will ask him
     for.
FW:  Is that right?  How do you like that?
     Do any of the girls or the guys you go around with speak
     any other languages like Spanish or anything?
IN:  No.
FW:  How about is there any white kids in your bunch?
IN:  Yes.
FW:  Uh huh. And uh, what would you rather be called:  Negro
     or colored?
IN:  Negro.
FW:  Any particular reason why you like that better than colored.
IN:  Just don't sound, just don't sound proper.
FW:  Okay good.  In this group you go around with, is there
     any one guy or girl that everybody listens to or the leader?
```

IN: No. Everybody to they self.

FW: Can new kids get in your bunch?

IN: Once in a while if we think they all right.

FW: How do they get in?

IN: Well they have to be cool and mellow and have to be hip
     to everything. They can't be the quiet type. That's
     all.

FW: Are you the quiet type?

IN: No.

FW: Good. What do you want to do when you finish school?

IN: Be a nurse.

FW: And what does a nurse do?

IN: She help sick people she do different things and she just
     help the people who sick.

FW: How long does it take to be a nurse?

IN: Four or six years, I think.

FW: If you had all the money you could ever want, all the
     money in the world, what would you do with it?

IN: I don't know.

FW: Uh come on, there must be some things you would like to
     do.

IN: I'd buy clothes. That's all.

FW: That's all?

IN: That's all. And maybe a house and furniture and a car,
     and get a put some money, enough in money in the bank for
     when I get grown I be able to go to college to be a nurse.

FW: Uh huh, good. Tell me what do you do on a typical day
     in the summer when school is out?

IN: Well...

FW: Describe it from the time you get up to the time you go
     to bed.

IN: Well when I get up, the first thing I do is eat breakfast.
     Then I put on my clothes, then I fix my hair then I do

my work then, I go outside then at 12 or about that time
I come in and fix me a sandwich and drink a pop or something like that or Kool-Aid then I go back outside and
I probably go over my girl friend house or I go upstairs
to the lady live upstair and we sits up there and play
cards and that time we play cards, that's all.

FW: Good. And what do they call this part of town?

IN: What what do they call it?

FW: Yes, do they have a particular name for this part of town?

IN: Nope. Not as I know.

FW: Where is the East side.

IN: Towards that way.

FW: They don't call this part of town anything?

IN: Call it the West Side.

FW: Okay. Good.

IN: Oh.

FW: What are some of boundaries to the town? Do you know any
boundaries? What's this city called?

IN: Detroit.

FW: Okay, what are some of the streets in Detroit, what
are the big ones?

IN: Grand River, Gratiot, Woodward, uhm.

FW: How about that one that goes by University of Detroit...

IN: Livernois.

FW: Uh huh, how about down by Cobo Hall?

IN: Uh. There's a street called State and that's the only one
I know down there.

FW: How about these big streets where you don't have any
traffic lights, what are they called? You can go real fast
in the car, 60 miles an hour, 55...what are they called.
You can get in the inner city real fast.

IN: What are they call?

FW: Yes.

IN: That's a street name?

FW: No. Is there any special name for that type of street?

IN: I don't know.

FW: Any of those you do think of?

IN: Nope. I know of a street you can go real fast on.

FW: Okay name some.

IN: Linwood and 14th, and 12th and 2nd and 3rd. That's all I know.

FW: How about, have you ever heard of an expressway or freeway?

IN: Yep.

FW: What are they?

IN: Well on an expressway well there's no traffic lights and you go down from, different ways you can go down, like on one street you go then about two streets and then you can go down another like that and there's no um traffic lights or nothing.

FW: And what are some of the expressways called in Detroit, can you name any?

IN: Edsel Ford, Lawton, John C. Lodge, and those the only two I know.

FW: Okay, good. Where were you born?

IN: In Detroit.

FW: Where else have you lived in Detroit?

IN: I lived on Seward, Byron, Euclid, Philadelphia and Bethune.

FW: Have you lived any place outside of Detroit?

IN: No.

FW: Where have you gone on trips?

IN: I went to Canada.

FW: Oh, what was that like?

IN: Well we went there with my mother cousin. We went there for the 4th of July. And we went in a cab to a

little place outside of, the river, uhm   the and we
sat there and played and ate.

FW: Good. What are some of the holidays that you celebrate
around here?

IN: The 4th of July, Memorial Day, Thanksgiving, Christmas,
Easter.

FW: What do you do on Christmas? How do you celebrate
that?

IN: Well we get toys and things like that, and we celebrate
by eating and that's all.

FW: Yes. Is there any special foods that you eat?

IN: And I eat turkey and chicken, and ham.

FW: Good. How about, what presents did you get last year?

IN: I got a science kit, a puzzle, two wallets, and clothes.

FW: What would you like this this year, anything you can
think of?

IN: A tape recorder.

FW: Is that right. To hear yourself huh. What about that
holiday around the end of October? What's that?

IN: Oh Halloween.

FW: Yeah. Ah how do you...what do you do Halloween?

IN: Well we dress up, you know, make ourself look different
and then put on masks and things. And we go out to houses
to house and say "trick or treat" and they give you something.

FW: Did you go out last year?

IN: No.

FW: Did your little brother?

IN: Yep.

FW: What was he dressed like.

IN: He dressed like a hobo. No, no he wasn't, he was
dressed like a little girl, I put him on my pony
tail wig, and put him on a long dress, and he had a

little shoes, and lipstick and earrings.

FW: And what did he say when he went to the door.

IN: He say "trick or treat."

FW: Anything he could say?

IN: That's all, I guess.

FW: How about those yellow orange things you can carve...
What are they called?

IN: You use on Halloween?

FW: Yes you can carve them out and put a candle in them
and make them look like a face.

IN: Pumpkin.

FW: Uh huh, good. And uh, what is the night before Halloween
called.

IN: Garbage can night.

FW: Is there anything else you call it?

IN: That's all I know.

FW: What kind of things do fights start around here?

IN: Somebody talk about them or tell somebody else what
somebody said. And come up and just start some...talking
about somebody said you said said something about them
or something like that.

FW: Uh huh, any rules for a fair fight?

IN: Any rules?

FW: Yes, for a fair fight.

IN: No you just fight.

FW: Did you ever get into any fights?

IN: No.

FW: Uh...

IN: Once in a while.

FW: Go on tell me about a good one you got in.

IN: Well I got in a fight with this girl named Katherine.
And she went around telling everybody, there's this boy
in my room named Anderson Hughes and he he wear glasses

and I call talk about him he ugly to me, and everybody
else think he look good but and I say he ugly. She
went around telling everybody that I go with him. And
she was so interested...I was talking to this girl, she
came up there and say, told her that I went with him
and so a fight, we started fighting.

FW: Do you scratch and kick?

IN: No I don't scratch.

FW: What do you do?

IN: Fight with my fists.

FW: Are you a pretty good fighter?

IN: Yeah, if I'm able to say so myself. I pull hair.

FW: Is that right? You pull hair?

IN: Yep.

FW: Did the other girl pull hair?

IN: Yep.

FW: Do they scratch and things?

IN: Scratch and kick and pull hair, that's just about all.

FW: Is that right. How about the boys, do they fight too?

IN: Yep.

FW: What's that like?

IN: Like being in a wrestling ring, in a boxing ring boxing.
     That's how they fight.

FW: Good. What do you say...

IN: Some...some boys, they fight like girls do, they fight
     with their hand and do like that and all like that.

FW: Uh huh. Good. What does the loser say when he doesn't
     want to fight anymore. Like what does he say when he's
     down, I don't want to fight any more.

IN: No. Like a teacher or some grown-up will come and break
     it up and they'd say, "the fight ain't finished" or
     something like that.

FW: Is there anything you can say if you know you've lost

and you say, I don't want to give any more...

IN: Just, you don't say nothing, I...I don't.

FW: Okay, good. Did you ever see anybody get beat up real bad?

IN: (Yes.)

FW: What happened?

IN: Well this girl was fighting with uh other girl, and she, they was fighting and she gave her a bloody nose and she made her, she broke the girl arm. She made her run into a tree and the girl arm be like that and she couldn't move.

FW: Yes. How about a boy, have you ever seen a get beat up real bad?

IN: No.

FW: Did you ever get into a fight with a girl bigger than you?

IN: (No.) Nope. I get into fights with around about the same size but not bigger.

FW: What was that like. Is she tough?

IN: Nope. Everytime I get into a fight with somebody they be smaller than me, the same size, but they be skinny or fat or something like that.

FW: And so you beat them huh?

IN: Yes.

FW Uh huh. Do the guys around here usually fight one to one or in gangs?

IN: Nope.

FW: How do they fight?

IN: Fight by they self.

FW: They never fight in gangs.

IN: (No.)

FW: Have you ever been in the hospital?

IN: Yep.

FW: Can you tell me about the worst illness you ever had?

IN: A broken arm.

FW: What was that like? How did you do it, what happened
    and what type of hospital were you in?

IN: Well we went, we was playing tag one day and this dog
    that live next door to us, it was a German Shepherd, and
    he jumped the fence and I had, we was playing tag and I
    ran backwards and fell on the rock and my arm hit the
    rock and I couldn't move it and I ran in the house
    crying and my mother took me to the hospital and we
    sit around there and they took X-rays and they said
    my arm wasn't broken but it needed protection and so
    I they put my arm in a cast and we sat there we didn't
    get home around 'bout after four o'clock in the morning.

FW: Did it hurt?

IN: Yeah it hurt and I had my arm my arm was swollen up.

FW: Uhm. Did you ever have any other bad illnesses?

IN: That was...my hand caught on fire.

FW: (When, why) was that?

IN: Well...When was it?

FW: Yes, what happened.

IN: Well my sister, my oldest sister say that one time she
    was lighting a, you know, putting some lighter fluid, in
    uh, uh, a lighter in her hand was still wet and she
    sent to light the, uh she went the light...lighter working
    uh, you know, the fire got on her hand and she said, long
    as the lighter fluid was in your hand it wouldn't burn you.
    So one night, she was going to do that and then the lady
    next door said, no don't do it. I went to the back door
    and closed the door and put some lighter, she told me to
    go and get the lighter fluid then she said she wasn't
    going to do it. And so I put some lighter fluid on my

hand and I kept putting it in there 'cause you know,
it dry up quickly. So then I put a match up to it and
then my hand caught on fire and my mother had company,
she had company, and I ran through the room and she saw
that blaze and my mother says to go through the door
she said, leave out of there. And I went in there and
my nephew and them was over and my nephew was taking a
bath and I went in there and he ran back toward the
bath tub and I stuck my hand in the water and I had
water blister all over my hand.

FW: Is that right. I bet it was painful, huh?

IN: It was hurtin'. Want me to tell you somethin' else?

FW: Yeah.

IN: And my, I scald my foot. I was over my sister house
and she uhm had went out and I was washing the dishes,
you know the glass coffee pot, I had put a bowl on the
stove and cut on the fire so it could dry, and I had
cut on the wrong iron, so I had cut on the water that
was in the glass coffee pot. So after I saw the water,
so I went to pour the water off, pour the water out,
and it was already cracked and I went to pour it off
and then the thing busted and it scalled my foot and
water blisters was on that. And I was the only one
home besides my nephews they were asleep and I called
my mother and she came over there rushing and then she
came back and my sister came back and I told her what
happened and she took me to the hospital.

FW: And what did they do there?

IN: They gave some kind of stuff to put on there and
they wrapped it up.

FW: Uh, huh. Ah, when a person starts to sneeze or cough
they might say ah...

IN: Achoo.

FW: Or they might say, get away from me I don't want to...

IN: Catch your cold?

FW: Yeah, good. Have you ever been in automobile accident?

IN: Nope.

FW: I bet you've seen one though.

IN: Yep.

FW: Tell me what, what was happening.

IN: Well, this man was coming down the street. It was in the night time and it was a lady and a boy and I guess they was arguing and this boy opened the door and jumped out and ran down the street. Then this other lady, she jumped out and she ran down the street. And the man lost control of the car ran into the light pole and the car caught on fire and the man was stuck in there. He couldn't get out. And he had knocked the pole over, the light pole and it was dark on the street and the they took a waited a long time to fix it.

FW: What happened to the man?

IN: He got burned   up.

FW: Did he die?

IN: Yep.

FW: Were you ever in a situation where you thought you might die or be killed?

IN: That I ever got killed?

FW: That you thought you might be die or killed or die.

IN: Yep.

FW: What was happening?

IN: Well I had the scarlet fever and my mother, we didn't know it and she called the hospital and they sent a man up there and they told me so as far as I thought I was going to die.

FW: What happened?

IN: He gave, he told me I had to be kept in the room by myself
and wash my dishes separate from the rest of them. And
they I get anything I wanted?

FW: Is that right? Sometimes people say that whatever is
going to happen is going to happen, how do you feel about
about?

IN: Now what you say now?

FW: Sometimes people say oh whatever is going to happen is
going to happen anyhow.

IN: Well I guess some of them just live right, that's all.

FW: Uh huh, okay good.

Interview No. 241

INFORMANT:...mostly they just make up little games. They
            watch TV mostly...not just regular games.

FIELDWORKER: [garbled]

IN: Well, we played mostly games outside, uhm, Jacob's
     ladder and so forth outside and then we would play in
     the house we played cards...oh, we played games like,
     uh...match games.

FW: How do you play Jacob's ladder?

IN: Oh, you hold your hands...up. No, that's London bridge
     isn't it. London bridge is falling down and then they
     had a Jacob's ladder and I don't really remember how
     you play that. And, uh, it's with a string...make a
     string and you make a ladder and you hold it up but
     uh...I forget and it was quite small. Oh, I have inter-
     ference. But, uh...kids mostly they just sit around
     and, uh, watch television or have guests ...oh, they
     like to play records and they like to dance. And
     they like to have a social. Like they get, uh, one
     friend each there's seven of them so they get one friend
     and they have a little party with Kool-Aid and cookies,
     mostly like that...Uh, John, I can't get him to sit
     still long enough to do too much...[garbled] fifteen,
     he likes to go swimming, uh, he likes, uh, basketball
     but he don't care for too many sports. He likes kickball,
     something like that...but not football and different
     things. He just love to swim...

FW: What's your favorite television program?

IN: Uhm...this will be funny. I like the, uh, Hillbillies,
     Flintstones, and I like I Spy, Long Hot Summer...I don't
     care for, uh, day programs...you know, the continued
     story...I don't care for those...I start watching TV
     about seven in the afternoon and I watch most of the

comedy and I watch, uh...most of the, uh, spy pictures
that comes on later. And Fugitive, things like that...
uh, they come on at ten o'clock, you know this is a
doctor that's supposed to killed his wife...and he
keeps running and he running. I watched him last night
and I watched I Spy and Long Hot Summer and I don't
like Peyton Place. And, uh...when Peyton Place come on
I usually try and find me some kind of detective story,
and I wind up on the comedies. On the Flintstones, or
something. Yeah...so...TV is...well, we got two so I
can go up and look at my program but TV is the most...
uh, center attraction at home...in this home. Uh, I
don't know about...the kids not having a father...it,
uh, don't give us too much outing...unless we go picnicking
and things like that which we do quite a bit of...(yes).

FW: What is the best movies that you've seen recently?

IN: Last time I went to the movie I believe I was seeing
double oh seven... and that was right around Christmas...
now I haven't been...I tried to get in to see Dr...Zagiva
...Zhivagi...downtown and you have to make reservations
to see that and I didn't get to see that...and I wanted
to see Maya before it leave. It's on now. But, uh,
double seven about the best one I...the last one I've
seen (yes).

FW: [garbled]

IN: Yeah, this was uh...uhm...I just remember what the, oh...
Thunderball, Thunderball that's the one. That one was.

FW: Is that the one where they try to steal that [garbled]?

IN: Yeah. (Yes.) They was trying to bomb someplace and they
had all this underwater fighting...and this cacoon boat...
I thought that was just wonderful...where, uh, you know,
he just got one big yacht and he says "shoot the cacoon"
and the boat comes right out of the back...and what have yo

got...you've got a, a a battle ship on the back, you
know, but it was just good...it was so way out till,
uh, it was way out...I enjoyed it though...I really
did...but the best movie I've ever seen in my life was
the Ten Commandments. Now I saw that about twice and
I want to see it again here but I didn't get a chance.
I thought that was nice. I don't go too often. Go to
church...Maybe occasional movies but nothing else.
(Yes.)

FW: Do you have any pets?

IN: Just a dog. Just a dog and...I don't care too much for
her but that's John's dog, but, uh,...I don't care too
much for running-around pets. I like, uh, the canaries,
goldfish...something that stay put where I put them you
know...when I got up keep up with a dog's seven babies.
I'm telling you, that's a job...so I don't. I don't care
for pets that much.

FW: Is there anyway that, when you were doing something,
anytimes that you more or less were obliged to make a
wish, like after you've been eating chicken and you
pulled the bone.

IN: You mean like the wishbone? Yeah. Broke the wishbone...
and made your wish and it's supposed to came true. Oh,
yea...I've had occasions to do that...they never came
true...they never came true. I wish all sorts of
foolish things, you know...but they' didn't ...I finally,
uh, come to the conclusion in order to make a wish come
true you got to be able to just about do it yourself. Yeah.

FW: And you know, some of the wishes I've made I'm really
glad they didn't come true.

IN: Me, too. Me, too. I think I'd have been gone long
ago if they had. I wanted to fly across the ocean, I
wanted to see the foreign land...those the type of wishes
I had.

FW: I had some nasty wishes when I was a mad at someone.

IN: Like wishing they'd drop dead or something.

FW: Exactly.

IN: Yeah. I've often thought of wishing that my mother
would just disappear you know...she'd get kind of
nasty sometimes and, and it was a secret...you just
close your eyes and make a wish and I'd say
when I wake up in the morning, and she wouldn't be here.
That'd be fine, you know. But I'm...those are the type
of wishes you don't want to come true. But it...makes
you feel better just wishing...It does...just to think
you can kind of do something about it, you know...

FW: Tell me about school. What was it like?

IN: When I was going to school? Well, I can say this much
about school...it's much different than today. I went
to school in Muskegon and it was pretty fairly large
school. First one I went to went up to the seventh
grade, kindergarten to seventh grade. Then I left
there and went to Jr. high, it had from kindergarten
to, uh, ninth grade. Then I left there and I went
to, uh, Central High and I stopped in the tenth grade...
but school to me was very nice. I really liked that
school but my people was kind of poor so I dropped out
of school. But school in my days was so much nicer than
these because you didn't, you could hear a pin fall, you
know, and when the teacher walked out the classroom you
were on your P's and Q's, you know...and when she came
back in you, uh, she would come back in very easy, very
quietly and you didn't look at her to watch, see if she
coming in or watch to see if she's going out. You mind
your own business and nowadays...soon as you walk into
the classroom you get a book thrown at you or anything...
so...I had a chance to talk to a principal about one of

the schools here. I haven't been here but a year see
and I told him, I said "sometimes you come by this
school and it sound like everybody's having gym."
That's just the way it sound...and they are classrooms
so he told me why the school was old and that...your
voice would carry when you talk...I understood that
part, I understood that part but, but, but, but, I
couldn't understand why you running down the halls
calling a boy on the other end of the hall or you
not walking orderly down the hall, we walked in two's
and they came in two's but these kids goes down
four, six, eight, come up the stairs in droves you
know so...school in my days was real nice I thought...
maybe the kids think they're nice nowadays, you know.
Maybe...they think mine is old-fashioned but I can
say this, what I learned I still got it. What they
learn they forget it by the time school starts next
semester. They really do...[To baby] Oh, I'm busy,
I'm going to clean house and I'm going to make 'em
worse a mess and if Mommy take that away from you I'm
going to scream...you can have it...I understand it's
quite a bit...I can't talk but I understand...okay stop.

FW: He looks lie he was playing [garbled]

IN: Yeah. Well, that's what he's doing. I got a great
imagination...but I'm a stinker at time...yea...

FW: Did you ever have a teacher who hollered a lot?

IN: Hollered a lot? No, I don't believe so. I had one
who was very, very stern. She was my favorite teacher
but I didn't like her. She, uhm...I liked...I, I, uh,
envied her, uh, but the way she handle herself, you know,
she was so sure of herself and just talk to you...but
she never let herself go. She was down to business, no
monkeying around and she, uh...well, she'd just straighten

you right out without even raising her voice. We didn't
like her because she made us work our heads off...but
really when you looked at it from the outside she was a
very nice woman...she was...she told me, she said "Alice".
I was seventh grade. She said "Alice"...I've always been
a bean pole, you know...she say "you're growing up to be
such a nice attractive little girl." She said "but I
want to tell you something, don't let this go to your
head." She was just this plain spoken, you know, and
she said..."if you keep the way you're going and always
smile, it'll get you a long way." That's been over twenty
some years and I never forgot it. She was just a nice
lady, but you get out of the way and she would just stop
and say "Now you know that isn't right; if you want your
ears pinned back I will do it." And you just...automati-
cally you got in your place, you know...she never touched
you...but now she would get hold of you...she'd pin them
back for you, too. But she was nice, her husband was a
teacher, she was a teacher. They had no children. Now
her husband is a truant officer and I really didn't find
out where she was when I went back...I wouldn't be a bit
surprised if she wasn't principal but she was very good
in anything...

FW: Do you remember a teacher that you just couldn't stand?
IN: Couple of them...really a couple of them. I had a science
     teacher and I couldn't stand her because she had snakes
     and turtles and all this in the classroom, and she would
     handle them and she'd want you to go up and experiment
     with (them) and I couldn't stand all these creepy bugs.
     And then, uh, as I think back I had one man teacher...
     come to think of, he didn't holler quite a bit. I mean,
     if he wasn't in on times he would start screaming about
     the door and when you sit down and, uh, if you couldn't

hear, very well, he'd start screaming about that...he
was, uh, well, now suppose you want to ask him a question,
you hold you hand...well, you just might as well forget
it's up there, you see. And if you go up to him half,
by the time you get half way, "what are you coming up
here for" you know. I don't even remember his name
but I believe he was my history teacher and I flunked
in history. So I think it was my history teacher.
I never got anything done in that classroom because he
couldn't...to me he couldn't express himself...he couldn't
explain what he wanted you to do. Well, enough. And
then if you wanted to ask questions...well, you should
have listened, you see. Yeah...so don't do that Lane,
stop Lane, stop.

FW: Did you ever play any trick on the teachers?

IN: No, not me. No. I was always a quiet student...I've
alway been the type of person to sit back and look. Now
I've seen many kids put tacks on the seats, you know, or
they take the test papers or something like this and hide
'em, they'd go in teacher's drawer and rumble it up, you
know. But I've always sit back and just watched them
and she'd ask who did it and nobody would tell so the
classroom got punished for it. But I, uh, never been,
well, I'm not bragging but I've never been mischievious
just to really get into something just because I could,
or because somebody put me up to it...uh, mother always
said I had a old-fashioned mind, I mind my own business,
sit back and watch you and if were wrong I'd leave you
right quick...'cause mother was very strict on us. She
would beat the daylight out of you, see. So now if the
neighbors would tell her we did something you'd get beat
half to death. If she found out you did something you
got beat half to death so, uh...she used to tell me all

the time..."Alice, no matter where you go, what you do,
I see you." And in this, in this town it had a tall
light up over the railroad tracks, you know, just this
big light after I growed up I knew...and she would tell
me, say "you see that light up there? I'm right up there
watching you." and that stayed with me until I grew up
and I, it came to me that that was the light for the
railroad station and that she was not up on that light
but anywhere I go...I said..."that light shines far and
I know she's watching me, and I can't do this." She
kept me pretty well in line till I got about sixteen and
she gave me a turn of heart, the boys could come and
see me and I could go. Then when I got so I could take
company she'd send my little sister along with me. So
I never had a chance to step out of line until I got
married. I came out of school...and the next year I
got married. So that's when my troubles began...all
my troubles. Oh, I was very happy at home, Well, as
much as a low income family can be, because I had a
stepfather and, uh, at that particular time she, I
can't remember too well how they got along except I
know they divorced about fifteen years ago and about
fifteen years ago is when I came out of school and
after I left home they divorced and so the home was
split up so I can't just say too much about it. But
for the last fifteen years after my oldest son was
born I got married, I've really been on my own so home
was never home no more...

FW: [garbled]

IN: Yeah. Once you leave I, I don't go back you know.
Because Momma says "you can't". Everything is "you
can't, you can't in my home you can't and as long as
you under my roof and you're gonna do this", well...

I'm thirty-two years old and I'm about gonna do what
Alice thinks and so I get my own house and I do just
as I like. So for fifteen years I've stayed in her
house twice...and the longest I've ever spent in her
house was one week...and I left. That's right. So I
could be free, you know. And like I tell my children...
once you get grown, you want to go, go. You free to
go, you know. Because...

FW: I think that's awfully hard to decide.

IN: It is. It is. But I force myself because I find if I
tell them to go they won't go...they won't. Put the
dog Lane...put it down. Uh, my oldest son, about a
month ago I got on him. I kind of roughed him up a
little bit. He was telling the boys out there that
one day he wouldn't have to listen to me, you know...
he's boasting off to the boys. About two weeks later
it got back to me. I brought him in the house and I
told him. I said now Junior, if you think you are grown
enough take care of yourself in those streets right now,
get your clothes and go, you see. There's the door, you
don't have to wait. Because as long as you're in my
house and I gotta see to you you going to do right...
I'm going to raise you way I think is right you going to
do it and you don't want to do it right now. I've had
no more trouble out of Junior no more. He'll tell you
quick...that's my Mother and I owe her a certain amount
of respect and I'm going to do it, you see, and they
say uh, man, what are you going to do when you grow up?
"Well, I think I be at home for quite some time. I
think I'll just, uh, just stay at home finish school and
if the service want me come and get me but I'll be right
here at home for quite some time." He changed his mind
see...'cause I don't care if he go...but if he had stepped

out the door I think I'd have fell dead, see. You see,
'cause I know he can't do it. But long as they think
you're going to cry and pet them they will just push
you now to give me this, to do this, to do that, but I
don't do it. I got too many and I want him to know he
got to stand on his own two feet. And ask me for advice,
I'll give it to him and if he do this he'll go right but
if he feels that he can make it, go ahead, make it. He'll
come home.

FW: What makes a person smart?

IN: What makes a person smart?

FW: Yeah.

IN: Well, I would say he's smart by being, well, first from
the beginning he's gotta be well-trained. The way I
think you become smart is your upbringing. If that kid
there, at the stage he is now I can teach him to do
anything. If I take a lot of patience and teach that
child, he's gonna be very intelligent. But if I let
the child raise himself by doing as he please, then it
seems to stunt 'em, they don't, uh, progress as early.
Now Veronica, this is a smart child here. Anything
she see done once or twice, she can do it again. John
is...slow in his books, but he's, uh, handy at doing
handy work or catching on to what mostly men enjoy.
But when it come to education I really don't think
John gonna make it. Uh, Veronica is slow. She's
the type of person, she likes to work in the home.
She's a clean neat girl. You don't have to keep behind
her. She know what she gonna do, she does it, she get
outa here. But when it come down to a book...it just
don't register. So really I think what makes you smart
is, uh, I didn't take much time with Veronica, either,
but with her she was the first girl, and all my time

that I could spend and doing things with her, I think it
helped her. With John, he was a boy and he was alone,
and I didn't take too much patience with him. I was
quite young when I had John. But this baby and the
baby before that baby...they're real apt...and, uh,
sometime the kids say "well, he's bad but I don't see
him being bad because anything he see one of those kids
do out there he'll do it, and he'll go upstairs and
wash his hand he might make a mess, but he'll wash 'em,
and he'll use toilet tissue. He's only three. You
tell him come downstairs and get something out of the
refrigerator he'll get it. But he's only three, but
they think he's bad, but I think he's...adjusted himself
quicker than they did. See? Okay. Stella can tell
him something and use a new word, he got it just like
that. You see? So I try to stop him. This is the one
I'm speaking of, and you can make him angry and he'll
run off in the corner and he won't say a word to you.
He's got sense to know it...yet enough to know how to
surl and...He won't talk back but he'll let you know
he don't like it. He don't appreciate it. That's what
I think make a smart child. The parents putting in a
lot of time with 'em. If they ask questions, answer it.
I don't care what question it is. If you (answer) answer
it intelligently, he won't take the wrong, uh,...attitude
towards it, or he won't think dirty of what you tell him.
Now, all my kids, down to the eight-year-old, as far as
life concerned, I tell'em. If they ask me, sometime they
stunts me, but I'll tell 'em. [Laugh] I get it out, you
know as telligent as I can...intelligently as I can, and,
uh, [to children in background] Stop now, stop! Stop!
Stop! Now the dog has had her puppies. Everybody know
this. Junior knows what to do for her and when and how.

He don't want to come in till..."the dog having puppies,
Mama." I say "is she?" You know. [Laugh] Of course I've
never noticed it, and right now if you sit down and talk
to him, you'll get a...they ask...they will, uh...express
themselves if they know that, uh, you're interested.
But my kid is a type of kid, if he think, uh, like John
said, out on the porch Mama, I don't need no doctor to
see. They...he thought you were some kind of psychiatrist
or uh, something like this. Yeah! And, uh, he didn't
want anybody...he say, well, they don't put you on cots
no more. They just talk to you to see if you're mentally
upstairs, you know. [Laugh]. So this is what I was ex-
plaining till he run around the back. He thought that's
what was happening. But if he think, well, you just
doing a survey or something like that he'll sit down
'n talk. Really, they, they're quick to think, you
know, and they're quick to pick up to things.

FW: [garbled]...was there a group of girls that you used to
go around with?

IN: No, not a group. Just one. We lived in a neighborhood.
We had, uh, quite a few girls, but I've always been a
person, to...I don't care for too many friends. So I
had my sister which is two girls and this one girl friend.
I would see the other girls. I would speak to them if
we were at a basketball game I would play with, but just
to visit their house or to go to the movies, go to church,
I only had one girl friend. Just like now. There's
people on all sides of me. I have one lady friend. I
speak to her when she's on her porch...her when she's
on her porch, that one right, right in front of me I
don't even know her. I don't speak to her at all. And
this one on the corner she is just another Alice. We
go to church together, we grocery together, we shop

together. I mean, we sit on the telephone. We call
each other five or six times, but anyone else they would
never get close to me unlessen I moved out the neighborhood. So I call myself sort of a odd ball. But this is
just the way I am. I just...I can't blend with people
because I'm not the sociable type. I can't keep a party
going, I can't...I can keep a conversation going with
people, but to be the ...as they say the...what they
call it?

FW: The life of the party?

IN: I'm not. I can blend in, in anything you do, I can, you
know, blend. But I can't start it or keep it going.
And I can't sing. I've never...I was good in school in
music, but I learned the notes. Most people now they
sing from the feeling, you know. I can't, what you
would say, ice skate, roller skate and all these things.
So that leaves me out quite a bit, uh...I like to bowl.
I like to sit up and watch ball games and things like
that. But just to go out and, uh, have a group of us
doing something, I wouldn't be good at it. You know,
just sit back and look.

FW: [garbled]

IN: Huh?

FW: You know, I mean, I'd feel left out.

IN: Well, I, I kinda do at times. I don't know why, but I
do. Uh, like most of the women, you know, they'll...
they'll visit and they can smoke, they can drink, and they
like to listen to records and they enjoy themselves. I
don't smoke, I drink very little, and I try to and I can't.
I've tried to smoke all kinds of cigarettes. I can't.
I tried to drink. I can't. I drink a beer or...one shot
lights me up. I find myself just sitting home listening
at the radio, watching TV. And I...I go to...I go to the

church. I enjoy myself. I go the movies quite often
...I talked to you about that. I enjoy myself, see.
I go over to her house, and we sit up and we talk.
But if we go to a stranger's house I find myself
clamping up, you know and I don't know. Maybe it's
something from way back that make me do that. But, I
do know one thing, you can't socialize with too many
women. Something always come up. See? And I say they
full of trouble...I stay away from those people, and
that has developed in me over the past years, and, uh,
if I see a person I...become introduced to them, the
first thing I see I try to analyze that person. I
try to see what type they are. If I don't like them I
leave them alone. It's just like that. But I don't
mean to be...yeah, I don't mean to be rude, but...I
do this automatically, you know. If I catch a real
intoxicated...it only have to happen once...maybe she
did it on her own, but, you know, if you intoxicated
I feel you stay inside, you know. I may be my door,
she's sitting out there intoxicated or something, it,
it does something to me, and I've got intoxicated but
...I was home. Didn't nobody know it. And, I don't
know, it's just the way I am.

FW: Let's see. What did you want to be when you were a
      girl?

IN: Well, it's way very far from what I became. I wanted
      to be a secretary or a nurse, and I didn't become
      either one...I worked a while as a nurse's aide, and
      I didn't finish school so I didn't become the secretary.
      But I always wanted to be a type of a person that would,
      uh, work and come home, you know. I've always dreamed
      of being a career girl, but I guess it wasn't cut out
      for me to be the career girl. I see to, uh, take care of

home and manage a home better than I can do anything
else. Uh, I found that I get awful bored when I work
two or three weeks and I'll quit. Now, I like to sew.
I sew very well. In fact, I can make anything I start
out to make from three-piece suits to evening gowns,
and I can sit at a sewing machine all day, half of the
night, and I can go out and work in an outside place
and get bored. So I guess I was cut out to be a home.
Uh, dreams wasn't really what I was cut out to be.
(Yes.)

FW: You aren't from Detroit, are you?

IN: No. (Yes.) I was born in Missouri, and I was raised in
Muskegon. I went to Muskegon when I was nine years old
...and I've been in Muskegon ever since, but for the last
two years. I went out to New York...spent two years, in
New York, then I came back here last year, but I find
that Michigan is about the most wonderful state that
you could live in. Uh, I haven't been too many space.
I've been to Chicago, Toledo, Cleveland, all around
Ohio, Illinois, and Indianapolis. Uh, I haven't been
in any western states yes, I've been in New Jersey...
Phillie...but out of all of them I'd rather be in
Michigan. They either hot, dry, the water's wrong...
the people in New York, I, I, I, I...they, they don't
seem human. They're...they're running, they're they're
they're, they're pushing themselves... and they're
always in a hurry to get nowhere. They're running over
the little man, you don't make any money, you don't, uh,
you can't advance, you in one little category...you stay
there. So I couldn't see myself getting ahead in New
York, so I said I'm going back. Here I can...I can
just about make out what I want to be, you know, as
long as it's within reasons. But New York they keep

you in one spot. They won't let you get out. That's
right. They keep you in a...renting place, you know,
if you want to rent a apartment, uh, apartment. Well,
you can believe you not gonna get an exclusive one if
your money don't call for. But here, you could save you
up a couple hundred dollars and for a week, live pretty
nice...not there...you can save up a couple hundred
dollars. That's just to get you in there, security
money you see. Well, where can I ever save five hundred
or six hundred just to spend a week, you see. They keeps
you pretty well in one category. So I came back here in
a hurry.

FW: And everything costs so much there.

IN: It does. Cost of living is above your head. Right.

FW: Let's see, how does your family celebrate the holidays?

IN: For the Fourth we got up five o'clock in the morning.
We left here at seven, went to the park and barbecued all
day, and, uh, we swang...we...teeter-tottered, we rode in
slides and the kids double-teamed and tried to beat me
up...[laughs] and they couldn't do that. We threw water
at each other. We just had...in other words, everybody
turned a child and we just had a nice time. Uh, I have
a car and, uh, when we don't go picnicking we'll go to
Toledo, out of town or we'll go someplace and see our
people, and, uh, we don't do too much of...way out,
but it's more of a family affair and we got quite a
large family. We get all the in-laws and everything
together, and we just enjoy quiet, you know, outing.
We have four or five cars and we strung out down the
highway. We find it it's pretty nice. The kids get
along quite well. They're large enough to understand
if I say the money's short and we can't go. We don't
go. Promise them another day and I'll take 'em. So

we've...we don't, uh, find that we're missing too much.
We could be missing some but whatever it is, we don't
know anything about. And I think the kids are reasonably
happy without a father and I'm reasonably happy trying to
raise them without one, because, uh, this way I can
tell the kids just about what's gonna happen without
someone else coming and interrupting my plans. And
whatever I, uh, plan to do I bring them all in the
living room...we plan together, and she'll take a job.
It's her duty to do this, John's duty to do that, in
other words. So it's working out pretty good although,
uh, all my people tell me that I should...before I get
too much older, try and, uh, get a companion because
after a while the teenagers are gonna be too old to
even think of marrying again. But what do you do, walk
out there and pull one out of the heavens, you know?
[laughs] Just don't come like that. You can't order
them in a mail order, you know. You can't...[laughs]
you can't just make what you want nowadays. You gotta
go through so many changes of finding him and I don't
have that will power. I just don't.

FW: What about Christmas?

IN: Christmas we had a great big Christmas tree and it was
     loaded with gifts from Muskegon, Toledo, Detroit, we
     had a great big dinner and a turkey and a couple
     chickens and all the trimmings. And, uh, where did
     we go on Christmas? I believe we went out of town on
     Christmas, or Christmas night we went out of town, and
     I'm a person like this. I love to travel. As long as
     I got a few dollars and a tank of gas I just might get
     up and say let's go, you know, and I tell the kids,
     you know, today I left about nine o'clock, well, I
     left earlier than that, I left at seven thirty so I

told the kids, well they didn't have to dress or anything.
They could put on some play clothes, but usually I try
to keep them in some pretty, uh, reasonable looking
clothes because I'm [garbled] get out there and get in
the car and say come on, let's go, I haven't time for
you to get ready you see. So we...we on the highway
most of the time and, uh, we go out to Belle Isle,
we'll go out to River Rouge, we'll go out to Plymouth,
we'll go way out just to look and ride and be together.
So I don't know if a man would fit in here anyway.
[laughs] He just might upset everything, upset the
apple cart, anything, uh, cause they're so used to,
Johnny so used to coming in saying, "Mama, I got
four boys, we'll give you a quarter." I say "that a
dollar, put it in the gas tank and let's go," you
know. Well, I might be cooking. I say in thirty
minutes let's go. I don't refuse them. See? And I
don't, uh, let nothing stop me from being with 'em.
So now I get a husband in here and...we gotta fix dinner,
we gotta do everything, you know, and I gotta put in
some time with him, and I think he would just upset the
apple cart. I think I'd rather stay just like I am.
Free, and I can do as I wish to do. But if I could
find one like me, got the same intentions I have, and
see I don't think it's supposed to be thataway. I
think it's supposed to be the woman's like him, you
know. But you know sometime the woman want him to be
like, uh, maybe both of them be...yeah, yeah, why
not! Let them be like us sometimes, and then maybe
things will run smooth, you know. Cause a lot of times
they...they ideas is kinda bumpy. They, uh, want to
put you somewhere you don't wanta be. And then if you
don't do what they want to do then they go in they acts, see

FW: What do you do for Halloween? Usually...especially the
    kids.

IN: Last Halloween I taking 'em all out except the babies.
    I taking a paper bag and put it in the pillow case and
    I, we just went from door to door and I just stood and
    watched 'em, and, uh,...well, we just trick or treat
    and come back home with it. That's all. And they enjoy
    trick or treating so I really didn't want to go, because
    I think we...it, it seemed to me we walked a hundred
    miles that night. We walked all over Detroit, you know.
    We were living on Seward, down in a rough part, so I'd
    taken 'em as far as Chicago...Boule...uh...street or
    boulevard or whatever it is, all the way back around
    Linwood, all the way back to the Boulevard back to Seward
    and I was beat. I was upstair...I was sick for about
    two days. [to children in background:] Get up now, get
    up. It's on his rug. Get up! Yeah. So just about
    every holiday, uh, we celebrate some kind of way.
    Memorials, we picnic...and we have my people over. Uh,
    my mother's house is small and she's so far away. My
    sister's apartment is small, and I have more space and
    room...my sister have six kids of her own, see. And
    when we all the kids together it's best to have a big
    place. So I've had four bedrooms upstairs and I have
    bunk beds in each bedroom, so it makes it kind of handy.
    Of course, we put the babies to bed, the kids to bed
    and we get some blankets and spread right out on the
    floor. So it makes it kind of nice when they all come
    here, but, uh, like I say I think we celebrate about
    every holiday except birthdays. Birthdays the adult
    get together and we just...have a birthday, little
    birthday reunion, it don't be a party, mostly we'll have
    a few drink and music and just us talking.

FW: It's nice to have a little time to talk.

IN: Yeah, yeah, just...just talk sometimes. And don't get
    out among them where you can't understand what they're
    saying and talking about. Course, uh, none of my family
    like, uh, night-clubbing and...if we go to something
    like this it's gotta be something like coming to Cobo
    Hall, you know. Some attraction coming in from out of
    town. But just on the weekends you see we go to a club
    or a bar. Well, we don't do this. We, we find it's
    cheaper to go to a store just buy what you want, come
    on home put some records on, turn the radio. We save
    money and then, when we get, uh, kind of woozie, we
    could relax, you know. But when you're out you gotta
    keep your poses, you gotta...keep yourself straight and
    you gotta...you can't look cock-eyed, and, you know.

FW: And you have to pretend you're having a good time.

IN: That's right. So how can you have a good time when you
    try to be something you aren't. So come home and get
    up in the chair here and just relax, and if you want
    to look kind of wild, then look that way, see. So we
    don't, uh, go in for all the big timing. We have fun
    just home. I think that's a good influence on the
    kids, too. Then when they grown they don't want to run
    the streets all the time. You find a lot of kids come
    from a going family that parties all the time. Well,
    Mom did it. My daddy did it, and he's living. He made
    it. But how did he make it. You know. So, uh, I
    rather them to...live a quiet life so when they get out
    there by on their own and they're making it, they won't
    think that what Daddy was making it doing this that and
    soforth and was making it easy because it's pretty hard
    sometime. And Dad don't tell you how hard he's having
    it out there. So I try, to, uh, get mine to understand

that whatever you do you've got to work for it and you
just gotta...things don't come out of heaven by, you
know, putting them in your hand. You gotta get out there
and get what you want. So they don't seem to think,
well, everytime they...in fact, I can go out the door and
they say "Mama, where you going now?" I can come home,
"You gonna leave any more today?" Well, it's Mom, I'm
supposed to be home, you know. And, uh, I...if I'm
going somewhere like this morning I tell 'em the night
before, because if I put on my clothes I gotta stop
and explain to seven people where I'm going, when I'm
coming back, what I'm gonna do. I'm thirty minutes
late, see, so I try...I try...I try to get along with
them more like, uh, people because I have to be so
many people. I gotta be Mama, Daddy, business, teacher,
doctor, nurse, so this way I try to win their confidence
by being everybody at one time.

FW: What sort of things do people fight about?

IN: Small things?

FW: Well, no. What do fights start about?

IN: Well, most fights I've ever known among the children,
     I have seen this...my children mostly. You know how
     children get outside and just talk, and one might say
     "your mommy's fat." That starts it with my kids. They
     can't stand nobody talk about their mommy whether you
     know her or not. And, uh, I find that kids will fight
     because some other kid bumped their little brother too
     hard. And I find that they will pick at each other by
     calling each other, uh, oh, all kinds of little names.
     "You're skinny" or "your eyes are big" or "you don't look
     right," you know. Among the grown-ups it varies. There's
     jealous people and a husband can't stand if you stay away
     too long. And where were you when I called you on the

telephone at two o'clock. [laughs] And the next door
neighbor's wife is looking at you a little bit too
strange, or you spending too much time over the you
lady friend's house. Well, I find that these things,
uh, keeps a home upset. Uh, I don't know. I've seen
'em where they come right down to a man just being so
insane jealous. He, uh, see that his wife looks very
attractable and go out and they have dinner. There's
a stranger over there looking at her and he swears by
heaven and hell that she knows him, is seeing him.
The poor woman knows nothing about him. So he gets
up and ushers her right out, you know. They get home,
they got the biggest brawls and two black eyes you
ever seen. So I have seen this happen but it's mostly
jealously in the adult. If it isn't that sometimes
children starts fights. Mommy spanked Junior and
Daddy didn't like it or Daddy spanked Junior and Mommy
didn't like it. I've seen that happen. So it varies.

FW: What do you consider a dirty fight?

IN: A dirty fight?

FW: Yeah.

IN: I consider a dirty fight is when, uh, a person is...
over average larger that the other person more experi-
enced and he's taking the advantage. For instance where
there's a man beating a...there's a man weighing two
fifty beating a woman ninety-eight pounds. And I think
that's dirty. Now I can see, uh, two boys fifteen years
old and the same weight fighting with their hands I
think this is all right I can see two fifteen-year old
boys fighting and one's got a knife, I think that's dirty.
I can see two mens fighting both of thems got a knife
and I think both of them's crazy. See? [laughs] No
feeling, that's right I just think both of them is crazy

because they're trying to kill each other and they know
that they're gonna die if one cut the other one so
they're crazy but just the right dirty fight is when
another person is taking advantage of a smaller person.
And know this person can't, well, he isn't just isn't a
match for him you know. As boxing I don't care too
much for boxing because usually it's very seldom they'll
put two good boxers together. They gotta put one there
that really knows that he can beat the other one up.
So I don't go in for boxing. Wrestling I used to like
until I found out it's all phony because if you trist
twist a man's arm and twist his head he's gotta show
some blood somewhere and they don't ever show any. So
how that's gotta be phony so I let that go, and sports
don't, uh, interest me unless they gotta be clean sports
...real clean sports. Uh, horse racing don't interest
me because a person can so easily fix a horse race.
It's gotta be clean. It's gotta be clean. Baseball
basketball I don't even like football. It look like
they're trying to bust each other.

FW: And they do!

IN: They do! They break collar bones they break legs, they
step on you with those spikes so, uh, I don't go too
far for any of that. Guess that's...they, well they say,
Alice, if, if everyone was like you, wouldn't be any
need for the world coming to an end. Well, it wouldn't.
Cause everybody'd sit at home minding their own business.
[laughs] They would just sit here look out that window
just like I'm looking now and mind it...because that's
as far as I get. This is my spot and I read my paper.
I read my books. I go to library and get my books,
and I sit right here and the neighbors tell me, "Why
you shut up in the house all day?" I like the house.

I try to fix it up where I can enjoy the house, and I
don't like to sit on the front porch. If it gets too
hot in here, I go upstairs and get the fan. And, uh,
they sit on the front porch, they see everybody, they
know everybody. I don't want nobody to know me. When
I walk out on the street I want to be different.
I'm just a odd-ball. That's all. But they sit there
till two o'clock at night. This is their enjoyment,
I guess. Well, I enjoy reading or...records or radio.
They get enjoyment out of sitting out speaking to people
that pass and different things. Like I'm not the
sociable type. But I find I stay out of trouble. I've
never been in jail, I've never been in jail, I've never
had any tickets, I've never had...to become involved with
the police. I've never had a fight with a woman. In
fact, that I've had a fight with a man, my first husband
slapped me on our wedding night. [laughs] That was the
end of that. He was, uh, full of booze, you know. We
were drinking. And he slapped me, but, uh, I figured
he didn't know what he was doing. I was trying to get
him in bed, and I just figured he didn't know what he
was doing, you know. But I just never, just, say, had
any kind of straight out fights. And I find if I mind
my own business I don't get into these things.

7: FIELDWORK EVALUATION

Complete homogeneity of performance with a new questionnaire
and transcription system cannot be expected from a group of
eleven different fieldworkers. In fact, any such claim
would generate suspicion. There is no general agreement
among linguists on what aspects of field work are most important, and what should be the strengths of the ideal fieldworker.
One may expect, however, that it is possible to assemble with
a high degree of confidence a group of fieldworkers who are
almost uniformly competent, but with varying strengths and
weaknesses.

Given the stated goals and proposed methods of operation
of the Detroit Dialect Study, it is possible in a general
way to assess the performances of the fieldworkers. What
is intended is not an evaluation of individuals as such,
but an organized assessment of the performance of the group,
which will be useful both as a measurement of the success
of the project in meeting its goals and as a reference for
other projects in the future.

The evaluators picked two tapes at random from those done
by each fieldworker in the second and fifth weeks of the
fieldwork in Detroit. This was done to minimize any bias
which might have been introduced by choosing only tapes
which were felt in some unspecified way to be representative
of the interviewers' best work. Consequently the particular
tape chosen may not be representative of the fieldworker's

typical performance, for reasons which have more to do with
the time, place, and informant than with the fieldworkers'
abilities, style of interviewing, or understanding of the goals
and methods of the Study.

The second week of the project was the time during which
the fieldworkers had had enough experience with each other
and with the interview and questionnaire to begin making self-
analysis improvements. At this time they were also arriving
at preliminary evaluations of each other's performance, and
preliminary evaluations and revisions of the interview questionnaire. This was, then, a time when fieldworkers were
still making adjustments in technique. The tapes from the
second week were included in the evaluation in an attempt to
discover those areas which could most fruitfully be stressed
in training fieldworkers for similar projects in the future.
The tapes from the fifth week, on the other hand, represent
a time when most adjustments in technique had been made.

A list of the important categories of the interview and
questionnaire was compiled, and the evaluators then ranked
the fieldworkers in relation to each other on a five-point
scale (see Fig. 15). Each evaluator scored four to six tapes.
No two tapes by the same interviewer were evaluated by the
same reviewer. As a check, the evaluators then exchanged
tapes, and points of disagreement were discussed and resolved.

Sections I through IV of the questionnaire were usually
covered on the first side of the tape, and Section V on the
second side. Also on the second side was the sample of the
informant's reading style and the various items of non-linguistic data which were necessary to correlate different variables
with speech phenomena. Since the general aims of the questions
on the first side were different from the aims of those on
the second side, the two sides were ranked separately.

EVALUATOR_____

TAPE NO._____

FIELDWORKER_____

SIDE 1   RANK

1.	Cues	1	2	3	4	5
2.	Interruptions	1	2	3	4	5
3.	Digressions	1	2	3	4	5
4.	Completing questionnaire	1	2	3	4	5
5.	Adaptability	1	2	3	4	5

SIDE 2

1.	Definitions of desired terms	1	2	3	4	5
2.	Allowance for variants	1	2	3	4	5
3.	Fieldworker cue sheets	1	2	3	4	5
4.	Adaptability	1	2	3	4	5
	Completion of interview	1	2	3	4	5
	Completion of informant data	1	2	3	4	5
	Suggested responses	1	2	3	4	5
	Minuteness of transcription	1	2	3	4	5

1 = Superior   2 = Good   3 = Average   4 = Weak   5 = Poor

Fig. 15. Evaluation Scale

Cues, the first category, is an evaluation of the interviewer's alertness to opportunities for eliciting further
narration and conversation from the informant. For example,
the following type of performance was rated superior:

FW: Do you play marbles?

INF: Yes, I have 197 marbles right here.

FW: Oh, tell me about them. How'd you get them?
What are the different ones called?

In other words, when the informant said something that indicated to the fieldworker that there was an object or event

in which the informant was interested, and about which he
might like to talk, the fieldworker attempted to elicit speech
on the subject. At the other end of the scale are such
passages as the following:

    FW: Did you ever play hide and seek?

    INF: Yes, I played that a lot.

    FW: What other games did you play?

Here the fieldworker missed an opportunity to elicit a description of the game of Hide and Seek.

    <u>Interruptions</u> are instances in which the interviewer asks
a question or makes a comment while the informant is in the
process of speaking. Since it is essential that the informant
be given every opportunity for extended discourse and narrative,
superior ratings were assigned to those interviews in which
there were very few interruptions or none at all. Lower ratings
were given when there was interference by the interviewer in the
stream of the informant's speech.

    <u>Digressions</u> are instances where commentary by the interviewer
seems to be unrelated to the effort to elicit speech from the
informant. For example, in the following passage, the interviewer seems to be conversing on the topic which is of interest
to him, and is not apparently intended to get the informant
talking:

    INF: ... automation, computers, and all that stuff.

    FW: Do you know how much these people are in demand now?
         That's something you should really know, you know.
         Beginning pay for computer programmers, for instance,
         which is not very--you should have math for a computer
         programmer--it's about six dollars an hour. That's
         what they charge at Michigan State University. It's
         pretty good, huh? How's that compare with what you
         get now?

    INF: Yes, quite a bit.

    FW: You just can't find computer programmers. I'd really
         encourage you to go into mathematics...

The fewer the digressions an interviewer made, the higher his rating.

The category called Completing Questionnaire is meant to indicate whether or not all the questions were asked in any given interview. Occasionally informants were so talkative, especially the elderly persons, that the interviewer was unable to cover the standard set of questions in the alloted time. This is not necessarily undesirable, except in terms of the attempt to achieve maximum comparability. It was on this basis that higher ratings were given to interviews which included all the standard questions and lower to interviews which did not, either because the interviewer forgot to ask some of the questions, or because the informant talked freely and at length without having to be urged.

One essential point that an interviewer must bear in mind in the collection of dialect material is that, in order to make certain that the informant's speech is as representative of his natural patterns as possible, there must generally be few or no outside influences, especially from differing speech patterns brought into the interview. This requires that the interviewer arrive at some preliminary understanding of the informant's natural speech, and attempt insofar as he can to avoid contradicting it. The category Adaptability is intended to evaluate the interviewer's success with this attempt. A negative reaction may be obtained from an interviewer's attempt to utilize speech patterns which are obviously not his own, but also a simple problem of comprehension may result from the failure of the interviewer to adopt speech patterns appropriate to the particular interview situation. The interviewer's questions and comments should not contain grammatical, lexical, or phonological features which directly contrast with the natural speech of the informant, nor should the interviewer explicitly question or contradict a form given by the informant.

For example, the following was given a low rating for adaptability:

    INF: ... and at the front is the chalkboard.

    FW: How come you call that a chalkboard? Don't you
          usually say something else?

Examples of high rated adaptability are the following:

    FW: Have you ever seen an automobile accident?

    INF: No.

    FW: Have you ever seen two cars crash?

    INF: Oh, yeah, I seen one just a while back ...

and:

    INF: ... she used to whup me.

    FW: What did she whup you for?

The category <u>Definitions</u> is related to adaptability, as discussed above. The definitions which were used by the interviewer to elicit the desired responses were ranked in terms of whether or not they were phrased in language which seemed to conform to the expected natural speech patterns of the informant, and whether or not they were phrased in such a way as to prejudice the informant's response toward a particular term or pronunciation. For example, a definition such as the following may bias the response toward one of the three possible responses: <u>postman</u>, <u>mailman</u>, and <u>letter carrier</u>:

    FW: Who is the man that brings the mail to the house?

A high rating was given to the following type of definition, which seemed invariably to get the idea across without mentioning any part of any of the possible responses:

    FW: When somebody writes to you, who brings it to the house?

<u>Allowance for Variants</u> is the category intended to cover the practice of asking whether the informant ever says anything else besides his first reponse. High ratings were given to those tapes where the fieldworker not only asked for other terms, but

also included them in his transcription of the second side of the tape.

Under the category <u>Fieldworker Cue Sheets</u> high ratings were given to interviews for which the transcribed sections either contained a separate sheet of remarks by the interviewer on impressions of the informant's speech and its peculiarities, or where such remarks were written on the short response form itself. A sample of a highly rated cue sheet follows:

Mrs. L.R. (WAW) Tape 406

FIELDWORKER CUES:

<u>The Interview Proper</u>: Although the informant was quite willing to assist in the interview, it was obvious that she was greatly handicapped in the speaking of English. It was difficult for her to put together more than two or three sentences in English. There was a large amount of phonological, lexical and grammatical interference. A number of items the informant only knew in Spanish terms with no English equivalent; on a number of items I also prompted her, since it was difficult to associate the description with a particular item. All places where I feel my prompting enabled her to get an item are marked. She switched to Spanish terms a number of times, particularly in the discussion when talking about childhood activities.

<u>Phonology</u>: The following types of phonological interference from Spanish were noted:

1. Use of unglided vowels: ['bɛdrumz].
2. Use of unaspirated voiceless stops: ['paŋkeks].
3. Use of [ɛ] (sometimes lowered), or [a], where [æ] is used in English.
4. Use of bilabial fricative intervocalically: ['beɓɪl].
5. Use of light <u>l</u> in all environments: [xɔ^l^].
6. Use at times of velar fricative for <u>h</u> in English:

[xɔ^l^]. (The informant's dialect of Spanish--
Mexican--uses an [x] instead of an [h] in some
varieties of speech.)

7. Use at times of flap r for a retroflexed r in English;
   at other times a variety of the English retroflex is
   used. Her retroflex, however, is further back in the
   mouth, has a certain amount of friction, and at times
   is voiceless.

8. Use of dental d and t: ['t‹ebɪl].

Morphology and Syntax: Several types of grammatical
interference were noted (only one example is given of each)

1. Omission of indefinite article: make wish.

2. Omission of passive auxiliary: I born.

3. Omission of modal: I help (for, I
                                      would help).

Impressionistically, there were other areas of interference such as double negative, use of present with past tense
context, etc.: however I did not note the examples while taking
the interview.

The remarks which applied to the category Adaptability
on the first side of the tape also applies on the second side,
except that emphasis was given to short responses from the
informant, since the aim was to elicit as many individual terms
as possible, to be used in studying the lexical and phonological
variety of the speech of Detroiters. Also more attention was
given to phonetic adaptability. It is questionable whether
repetition of the informant's response by the interviewer is
necessary or even a good idea at all. When interviewer's
repetition embodies a pronunciation different from that of the
informant, it seems to imply a contradiction by the interviewer
of the informant's response, and as such is undesirable. A low
rating was given, for example, to the following:

FW: What do you call the thing that keeps the rain out
    of the house?

INF: /ruf/.

FW: Oh, /rʊf/.

The remaining categories apply to the overall interview.
High ratings for Completion of Interview were given to those
tapes which included all the questions from all sections of
the standard questionnaire, as well as the reading and any
questions the informant had for the interviewer. Under
Informant Data, high ratings were given for the inclusion on
the tape of answers to all the questions about non-linguistic
status of the informant, such as place of birth, race and so
forth.

Since there were a certain number of short response
questions on both sides of the tape, the category Suggested
Responses applies to the overall interview. A low rating would
be assigned to the following:

FW: What's the kind of white stuff that women who diet
      have to eat a lot of? Curds. It's a kind of cheese.

INF: Cheese.

FW: This is white, you probably don't think of it as a
      cheese, though, cottage cheese.

INF: Oh, yeah.

FW: Do you like that?

INF: (No.)

FW: Could you say that for me just once?

INF: Cottage cheese.

FW: Have you ever heard it called anything else?

INF: (No.)

FW: Like smear-case or Dutch cheese?

INF: Well, once in a while I hear of it, but mostly it's
      cottage cheese.

FW: You do hear it called Dutch cheese once in a while?

INF: Just once in a while, but usually cottage cheese.

FW: (Yes.) Or pot cheese, you won't hear it called...

INF: (Yes.)

FW: Do you hear pot cheese, too?

INF: I haven't heard pot cheese, just Dutch cheese.

FW: Would it be around the house or from your friends?

INF: Cottage cheese?

FW: No, Dutch cheese.

INF: Uhm, from my friends.

FW: That's not so usual in this area, they use it further
      east.

In the preceding passage, the interviewer seems so desirous of
getting Dutch cheese or pot cheese, that the informant, who is
trying hard to please, seems to have been forced into admitting
a term which he may very well never have actually used. Lower
ratings were also assigned to those tapes where the interviewer
suggested a response outright, or showed the informant a written
word to have him simply pronounce it.

An indication of the range and average value of the Minuteness
of Transcription is given in the final category. One page of the
transcription of the Short Response section was examined for each
of the interviews evaluated. A page was selected which generally
had elicited a response for each item, and on which the responses
were nearly always the same terms. Instances in which a response
was omitted by a fieldworker were compensated for by assigning an
average value on the basis of the other fieldworkers' notation.
The total number of different symbols used in the transcription
was then tabulated for each interview, and the figures for the
two interviews of each fieldworker were averaged. The total
seemed naturally to fall into five groups (see Fig. 16).

These figures are not intended as an evaluation of the perception of the interviewer or his ability to transcribe phonetically. A number of uncontrollable variables, such as the inform
ant and the quality of the tape recording, obviously helped to
determine what figure was arrived at for any particular tape.

WKR	119.5	1
JL	108.5	2
WAW	106	2
REC	102	3
JWN	102	3
EAA	101	3
RKS	99	4
CMW	98	4
DD	97.5	4
VHL	92.5	5
CWJ	90	5

Fig. 16. Minuteness Ranks

In order to characterize more explicitly the nature of the differences between different transcribers, a tabulation was made of the number of kinds of symbols used by each fieldworker during the second and fifth weeks, respectively (see Table 3). The tabulation shows the number of types, of vowels, diphthongs, and lateral consonants used by each fieldworker in these two interview weeks, and the number of tokens for each of the other categories. This reflects the fieldworker's personal assessment of what in his data is phonologically interesting and relevant to the study of phonological variation in urban speech. For example, one fieldworker never marked stress at all, but consistently marked fronting, raising, lowering, and backing vowel modifications, as well as length. The number of words missing from the page checked is included since some of the missing or infrequent symbols might have occurred had these words been elicited.

Table 4 shows the relative ranking of fieldworkers by categories for the second week (upper row) and fifth week (lower row) of interviews. The figures indicate the number of fieldworkers within each specific rank. The figures for

Table 3

Number and Kinds of Symbols Used by Each Fieldworker: Second and Fifth Weeks

Field-worker	Week	Types: vowels	Types: diphth.	Types: lat.	Tokens: stress	Tokens: < > ‹ ›	Tokens: nasal	Tokens: length	Tokens: voicing	Tokens: lenis	Tokens: ʰ, >, ˒, ⌐	Words missing
EAA	2nd	7	4	1	6	7	1	2	2	2	4	
	5th	8	3	1	10	7	6	9	2	1	8	
REC	2nd	7	3	1	11	2		9	1		3	
	5th	9	2	1	11	1		6			3	1
DD	2nd	7	6	3	11	10	1	1			7	
	5th	3	7	1	9	4	1	1			3	3
CWJ	2nd	8	3	1	13	6	1				3	
	5th	6	3	1	9	4	1	1			3	
RKS	2nd	9	3	1		10		2			1	
	5th	9	6	1		16	6	4			2	1
JL	2nd	9	7	1	2	25	2				6	
	5th	5	7	1	7	17	4		3		9	1
VHL	2nd	8	4	1	9	1					6	
	5th	8	4	1	7	2	1		1		5	2
JWN	2nd	8	4	2	12	9			2		2	
	5th	6	4	2	12	11			1		3	2
WKR	2nd	7	7	2	13	14	9		1		6	
	5th	5	9	2	12	18	8		5		5	
CMW	2nd	8	4	2	20	1		3	1		2	
	5th	8	2	2	10		1				4	1
WAW	2nd	7	5	3	5	4	7	2	1	1	7	
	5th	10	1	1	14	14	1	1	3	2	4	1

Table 4

Evaluations in Categories: Second and Fifth Weeks

RANK*

Category	1	2	3	4	5
Cues	2	5	3	-	1
	5	2	2	2	-
Interruptions	5	5	1	-	-
	3	3	2	2	1
Digressions	9	1	-	-	1
	3	4	2	2	-
Completing Questionnaire	9	1	-	-	1
	3	4	2	2	-
Adaptability (Side 1)	3	2	3	2	1
	5	2	2	-	2
Definitions	2	5	3	1	-
	3	4	4	-	-
Allowance for Variants	1	3	6	1	-
	1	3	6	1	-
Cue Sheets	-	-	2	3	6
	3	1	-	3	4
Adaptability (Side 2)	4	3	3	1	-
	4	2	4	-	1
Completion of Interview	11	-	-	-	-
	3	6	1	1	-
Informant Data	5	3	2	-	1
	4	4	3	-	-
Suggested Responses	3	2	3	1	2
	-	4	2	3	2
Minuteness of Transcription	1	2	3	3	2
	1	2	3	3	2

*Upper row: 2nd Week; lower row: 5th Week

Minuteness of Transcription represent an average of the two
weeks and hence are the same for both rows.

Several areas of general improvement seem to reflect an
increasing facility with the standard interview. One such

area is that of Cues; another is Adaptability on side one of
the tape. Interruptions and Digressions generally decreased
from the second to the fifth week, as did the rankings for
Completion of Interview and Completing Questionnaire. The
latter two may reflect a growing feeling of freedom among
the interviewers to elicit discourse where possible with a
minimum of questions. Cue Sheets were more often submitted
in the fifth week than in the second, and Definitions seem
to have generally improved.

The categories in which there are several persons with
ranks of 5 would seem to be areas where further explicit
training of future fieldworkers might be profitable. This
is also true for one or two categories in which the rankings
seem to be generally lower in the fifth than in the second
week, e.g., Suggested Responses.

In conclusion, it should be noted that for both weeks
a number of the fourth and fifth rank spaces are blank, and
large figures occur in the first three ranks. It is believed
that this fact indicates that the overall quality of the
fieldwork of the Detroit Dialect Study was quite acceptable.